Using Restorative Circles in Schools

Using Restorative Circles in Schools

How to Build Strong Learning Communities and Foster Student Wellbeing

BERIT FOLLESTAD AND NINA WROLDSEN

Foreword by Belinda Hopkins

Jessica Kingsley *Publishers*
London and Philadelphia

First published in Norwegian in 2017 by Fagbokforlaget
This (English language) edition published in 2019
by Jessica Kingsley Publishers
73 Collier Street
London N1 9BE, UK
and
400 Market Street, Suite 400
Philadelphia, PA 19106, USA

www.jkp.com

Library of Congress Cataloging in Publication Data
A CIP catalog record for this book is available from the Library of Congress

British Library Cataloguing in Publication Data
A CIP catalogue record for this book is available from the British Library

ISBN 978 1 78592 528 3
eISBN 978 1 78450 917 0

Printed and bound in the United States

Contents

Originally published in Norwegian, this edition has been updated with new material and written under great inspiration from Belinda Hopkins.

Translation of original material undertaken by Nina Wroldsen.

We send warm thanks to enthusiastic colleagues and brave students for sharing their experiences with us. They have taught us a lot.

Foreword

Belinda Hopkins

It has been an honour and delight to work with Berit and Nina over the years, sharing our enthusiasm for restorative approaches at many of the stimulating conferences run by Tryglarung, the organisation they co-founded with other passionate Norwegian educators. These conferences have always been joyful events, which usually begin by using circle process with everyone present to build a bonded learning community amongst conference participants. In other words the authors have demonstrated how well circle activities can work to break down isolation between people who have not previously met, how shared fun and laughter can create connections between people, how opportunities to participate in pair and group discussions can help people overcome their nerves at meeting new people. How wonderful it would be if all conferences began in this way!

It is with great pleasure that I am now able to support them further by encouraging people to read their book on restorative circles. This is a book that has grown out of their experience implementing restorative practice in many schools across Norway. This experience shines through, not only in their anecdotes and confident explanation of how to facilitate circles of different sorts but also from their deeply grounded understanding of why these practices are so needed, not just in Norway but in schools across the globe.

The book is timely —the health and wellbeing of young people, and of those who work with them, is a live issue, as is the continued concern about the safety of young people as bullying, violence and radicalisation threaten their daily lives in and out of school. Nina and Berit also explain the importance of the psychosocial environment on learning, an issue that again becomes ever more important to educators as our understanding of brain development increases.

The book advocates using circles of all sorts to build strong caring communities within classrooms, and amongst staff teams, and thereby create the foundations on which a school culture based on relationships and connection can be constructed. Berit and Nina share ideas for games and lively activities that encourage participants moving around, sitting next to and talking to different people, working in pairs and small groups and always coming back to the full circle to reflect on what has been enjoyed and learned. These activities develop a range of relationship skills that can then be harnessed, if and when necessary, to put things right when they go wrong.

In light-hearted ways pro-active circles provide an opportunity for people learn to listen to what others are saying; reflect back what they have heard; develop empathy and understanding for what it is like to see the world differently; to develop a vocabulary of express emotions and needs; to practice negotiation and co-operation and to experience the joy of feeling included and connected. And these are the very skills that will be needed to put matters right when they go wrong and to repair the harm done to the complex weave of relationships that make a school a safe caring place. This book provides plenty of examples of how to create the foundational elements of a restorative school – the values, the principles and the skills – and also examples of how these values, principles and skills can be used to address challenges and conflicts.

The book provides very practical ideas to classroom teachers. Perhaps I can offer some hints for the school leaders who will be creating the framework in which their staff can run the circles.

I have been privileged to support inspirational school leaders to introduce restorative approaches in their schools and travel with them along their implementation journey over many years. I have seen how vital the role of the senior leadership team is in setting the example – themselves using circles for their own team meetings, and encouraging departments or facilities to also hold meetings in circle. The key to success here is every participant abiding by the 'talking piece' rules – the piece passing around 'with the sun' (clock-wise) as Berit and Nina describe it, with no-one talking if it is not in their hand, no-one interrupting until the piece comes back to them around the circle and crucially, listening with an open mind and an open heart to whatever is being said. This is not about agreeing with all that is said necessarily, but about being open to appreciating differing perspectives and seeking to understand why someone may have a different view from ones' own. Countless school professionals have told me how this regular practice with colleagues has transformed their team culture.

The second hint for school leaders is – make it possible for circles to happen and support those members of staff who are not natural facilitators. Perhaps alter the school timetable as some schools do to allow for weekly circles to take place. Encourage staff to share their circle programmes and ideas so that creating them does not become another onerous task. Sit in with timid or more traditional members of staff for whom facilitating a circle may feel initially worse than having deep root canal dental treatment and co-facilitate until they feel more confident or more convinced.

A third hint would be to make explicit links between your Teaching and Learning Policy and the active, participative techniques of circle practice. Negotiation, dialogue, collaboration, pair and group work – these are all tried and tested pedagogical techniques and circle process utilises them all. Also emphasis the affective domain – good teaching and learning harnesses the thoughts, feelings and needs of all learners and so it is possible to bring so-called 'restorative' questions into academic teaching. Offer in-service guidance so that all staff can make these links.

Fourthly establish a staff committee to support their colleagues in implementing circles and check-in with what extra support, information, resources or training might be needed to keep up the momentum. This committee can also monitor the impact of regular circles on staff and student health and wellbeing, engagement, motivation and happiness.

And finally – buy a copy of this book for every department or faculty or better still for every member of your staff! It would be an investment you will not regret and your staff and students will thank you for it.

Dr Belinda Hopkins
Director of Transforming Conflict, the National Centre for
Restorative Approaches in Youth and Community Settings
www.transformingconflict.org

Introduction

Put simply, a restorative circle is a community process for supporting the members of a group, which facilitates communication based on dialogue and active, equal participation.

Restorative circles in schools provide participating individuals with time and space to listen, and with opportunities to develop their attention span and oral communication, and to learn new concepts and skills. They can also be used to explore auditory memory and sensory experiences, to encourage socialisation and, importantly, to have fun!

When used in the right way, they can be used as a tool to help to create safe and inclusive learning environments.

WHY THIS BOOK?

We decided to write this book because we want to share our experience with the use of restorative practices and to give the reader an introduction to a theoretical and practical framework for building and repairing strong working relations between students and between students and teachers. This book presents the reader with an accessible explanation of restorative thinking along with practical methods that can be used both proactively and reactively.

We have written it for anyone who works with children or young adults, and intend for it to be a concise and useful book for practitioners – throughout the book, text is accompanied by figures, stories and authentic interviews.

INTRODUCING THE AUTHORS

Berit Follestad is an educational counsellor and trainer in the field of restorative practices, and has more than 20 years of experience as guest lecturer at universities in her native Norway and internationally.

Nina Wroldsen has taught in secondary schools for several years and works as a school leader of a new international primary school programme that employs a whole-school restorative approach.

Berit and Nina are also co-founders of Safe Learning Norway, an organisation that promotes the use of restorative practices in schools (www.trygglaring.no). Their experience is mainly derived from teaching in larger multi-ethnic inner-city schools comprising a diverse student body with more than 100 different first languages spoken.

The cases and the interviews in this book are drawn from both primary (4–11 years) and secondary education (11–18 years).

RESTORATIVE PRACTICE AND STUDENTS – THE CONNECTION BETWEEN POSITIVE LEARNING ENVIRONMENTS AND STUDENT WELLBEING

The psychosocial learning environment is important for how students experience their school situation. The most important factor is the social interaction among students and between students and teachers. A good psychosocial environment promotes students' health, wellbeing and learning. Student wellbeing can be defined as students' overall development and quality of life. The Programme for International Student Assessment (PISA) survey in 2015 investigated students' wellbeing and their sense of belonging to a school community. PISA is an international comparative survey of the educational school systems in different countries initiated by the Organisation for Economic Co-operation and Development (OECD). PISA measured 15-year-olds' competences in reading, mathematics and scientific literacy, as well as students' well-being. In 2015, 72 countries participated in the survey. It reported that students who feel they are accepted and liked by the rest of the group and feel connected to others and part of a school community are more likely to perform better academically and are more motivated to learn (PISA 2015, vol. 3).

All students have the right to attend schools that promote their well-being, but how can schools create this environment? Teachers, both newly trained and experienced, need a tool to help develop a positive psychosocial learning environment.

Our belief is that the use of restorative circles can provide schools with a method to achieve an engaging and active learning environment that promotes students' wellbeing. The use of restorative circles could help reduce exclusions according to the Restorative Justice Council (Weale, 2017).

STUDENTS

An increased focus on a learning environment that promotes students' wellbeing has arisen alongside the increased use of social media and the growth of new forms of bullying, often described as 'cyber-bullying'. Cyber-bullying as a term can encompass the sending of malicious emails, spreading rumours, posting photos on the internet without consent or excluding students from online social groups (O'Moore, 2016).

Students' wellbeing is also tied to a range of other pressures to which children and teens are typically exposed.

Children in schools today are sometimes labelled 'generation perfect' due to the pressure they feel to strive for perfection. This can affect children at a very young age.

Young people complain about the pressure in modern society. They feel under pressure to be good looking; to be skinny and fit. They face pressure from peers to be popular and to have an exciting social life. They also face pressure from parents to succeed in school.

Official reports from the Norwegian Directorate for Children, Youth and Family Affairs have indicated an increased number of young adults experiencing mental and physical illnesses, which are attributed in part to such pressures, and the suicide rate among teens is on the rise.

According to statistics from the World Health Organization, suicide is the second most common cause of death among young adults between 15 and 29 years old (WHO, 2017). The high suicide rates may be caused by several factors besides pressure and raise concern around a global phenomenon, but the point here is to point out a global phenomenon and raise a concern.

Another concern is students' disruptive behaviour and teachers struggling with classroom management and noisy classrooms. By way of example, PISA has reported that '…about one in three students reported that in every or most science lessons students do not listen to the teacher or that there is noise and disorder...', and that some 4 per cent of students are hit or pushed around by other students a couple of times per month, and 11 per cent report that other students make fun of them a few times every month (PISA, 2015).

What causes this challenging behaviour? There is no single answer to this but several factors are involved.

THE SCHOOL ENVIRONMENT

Conflicts that happen outside of school (bullying, violence or arguments with friends or family) are often brought into school and may cause upset and disruption. Such conflicts can lead to negative social learning environments, which in turn have a negative impact on the students' wellbeing and academic performance.

How can schools help students resolve conflicts and thereby improve the learning environment?

We cannot become good people without the presence of others.

Niels Christie (2009, own translation)

Good psychosocial learning environments can strengthen students' sense of belonging to the school community and in doing so can be crucial to prevent negative behaviour. A good school environment and community can help to guard against alienation, social isolation and disaffection that can lead to extremism, radicalisation and, at the very extreme end of the spectrum, acts of violence such as school shootings. There are several reports from schools where violence has been reduced as an outcome of using restorative approaches systematically over a longer period of time.

THE ROOTS OF RESTORATIVE CIRCLES

The use of restorative circles has evolved differently in different parts of the world. In Norway restorative circles are used in both primary and secondary schools. Most schools practise a whole-school approach using restorative circles as part of a daily or weekly routine. Very often, these schools also practise student-to-student mediation.

New Zealand has played a pioneering role in incorporating restorative practices into its justice, welfare and educational system, and restorative practices have become established as a global social movement for the creation of a more democratic, caring and peaceful society.

In Brazil, Dominic Barter, inspired by the practice of Nonviolent Communication – an approach to non-violent living developed by Marshall Rosenberg beginning in the 1960s – implemented restorative circles in the mid-1990s in the favelas, and the practices he pioneered continue in Brazil and in Brazilian schools and have also spread internationally. Barter has been awarded many prizes for his work and is a pioneer in the field.

However, two of the authors' most important inspirational sources have been the organisation Transforming Conflict in the UK, founded by Belinda Hopkins (www.transformingconflict.org), and the work of Ted Wachtel, the former principal of the International Institute of Restorative Practices (IIRP) in Bethlehem, Pennsylvania, USA (www.iirp.org).

In this book we relay the wisdom and experience of these influences to provide you with the knowledge and skills you need to create safe, inclusive learning environments and teach life skills in your school.

A NOTE ON LANGUAGE

In this book we use the terms 'restorative circle' and 'circle' interchangeably.

In the field of restorative practices there are many words and concepts being used. Here is a diagram of some of them:

Fig. 1 Concepts

Part 1

Restorative Circles – a Mindset, a Method and Tool for Conflict Resolution

Fig. 2 Group of teens

As explained in the introduction, a restorative circle is a structured way of enhancing safe communication and to develop social wellbeing and strengthen social competence and social skills. It's intended to encourage participants to talk *with* and not *to* each other, while listening carefully to one another. Restorative circles are used proactively but also reactively to address problems that arise.

So what does a restorative circle look like?

Participating students sit in a circle and the teacher or adult – acting as the facilitator – sits in the circle with the participants. This way, all participants are facing one another and can see each others' faces directly. Everyone gets equal attention and can learn to trust each other and feel safe; no student can hide or be the centre of attention, and everyone is able to participate as equals and be respectful to one another. All voices are heard and they all must listen to what the others are saying – without comments or interruptions.

The goal is to have the students open up and recognise that they have a lot in common with their classmates. The result is a safe atmosphere and good relationships, both between students and between students and teachers.

The method is also used reactively and schools can rapidly adapt restorative practices as an alternative and/or supplement to the punitive justice that has been used in schools for misbehaviour to replace the traditional disciplinary sanctions. When misbehaviour occurs, it affects everyone in class and the teacher facilitates a problem-solving circle to address the problem. This gives every student an opportunity to say how they are affected and how they feel about the misbehaviour, and how they would like the future to be.

Can students be trained to facilitate circles – both proactive and problem-solving circles?

We have found that it may be fruitful to train the class representative to facilitate circles. The teacher participates in the circle as well both in proactive and reactive circles, and is given the opportunity to express how the misbehaviour has affected his or her teaching. Hearing how the teacher has been affected by what has been going on in class can have a great effect on the students. In that way the teacher models how to communicate to improve the classroom atmosphere.

> If we are not modelling what we teach then we are teaching something else.

> *Helen Flanagan*

The feedback we receive from students indicates that a restorative circle facilitated by a class representative is more effective than a teacher-facilitated circle. The students feel they can speak more openly when a peer leads the circle and the communication is more honest. The main goal of a problem-solving circle is to speak openly and come up with suggestions for how to repair the harm. It is important to focus upon a few points for improvement to avoid any future misunderstandings. We usually invite the participants to a follow-up meeting later on, for instance, after two weeks. Students have reported back that they appreciate this way of repairing harm; that they have learnt a lot from each other and they feel more empowered and empathic, open and safe, which are some of the core values in restorative practices.

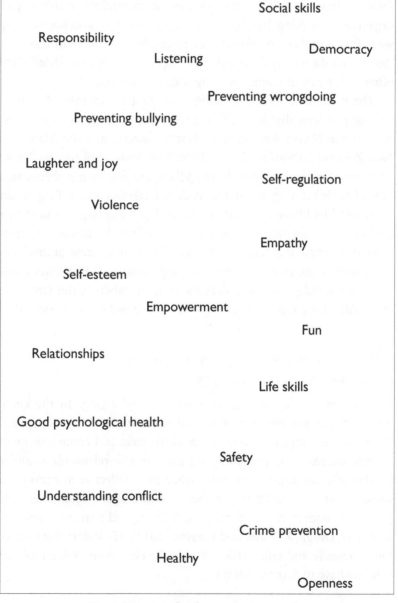

Fig. 3 Concepts related to restorative practices

CIRCLES – AN ANCIENT TRADITION

To gather in a circle is an ancient tradition used by different peoples around the world when there is a need to talk and find solutions to situations that have occurred. Our forebears gathered in circles for many purposes: around the camp fire to share the day's hunt, when important decisions were to be made or when conflicts needed to be resolved. In other words, there is something natural about this way of organising a meeting, but for various reasons modern man has in many ways forgotten how or chosen not to conduct meetings in this way. How often do we organise staff meetings by sitting in a circle? How often is this way of communicating used in classrooms?

The method is rooted in indigenous peoples' traditional way of solving problems that have affected members of the local community, such as the Native Americans in North America and the Maoris of New Zealand (Johnstone, 2002). From Scandinavian history we know a variant of circle meetings. In the Viking era free men gathered in a type of circle meeting, a common collegial meeting at the 'Ting' when a bad deed had been committed. The collegial meeting was held in a confined area, for instance, in a village. Before the meeting started, a band or rope was laid out/stretched out in a circle around the exact spot of the meeting. The band/rope constituted an inner circle dividing the judges, the offenders and other members of the Ting. The inner side of the rope was sacred where peace and justice prevailed.

CIRCLE – A SYMBOL OF COMMUNITY AND RESTORATIVE VALUES

To participate in a circle gives a sense of belonging. In the circle everyone can see everyone else and takes turns in speaking, and what everyone says everyone can hear. To meet and communicate in a circle increases the possibility for positive safe relationships and a psychosocial atmosphere best described as a collective attention – a sense of 'we'. In classes where there are safe relationships there are positive classroom environments, less bullying and a stronger sense of unity (see Drugli, Klökner and Larsson, 2011). How does the teacher build inclusive and safe relationships in the classroom? What tools do teachers have to accomplish this?

In our experience, students who participate in a circle on a regular basis will less frequently turn to bullying and other forms of undesirable behaviour. Instead they create an environment with a stronger sense of unity and cooperation. What are the reasons behind this? Let us have a look.

The way the process is conducted makes the circle a symbol of community and conveys core values such as equality, safety, trust, responsibility, justice and democracy.

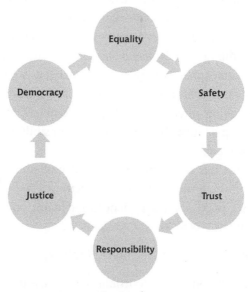

Fig. 4 Values

The work is focused on relationships and it mirrors the reciprocity of the mutual responsibility between the individuals and the community. When the teacher starts using circles as a daily routine proactively this will promote an inclusive and good psychosocial school environment. Students often ask: 'Can we do more of this?' This indicates that the circle method engages and inspires participation and an active classroom community.

Restorative circles emphasise learning by doing; that is, active participation, sharing of experiences, activities, role plays and reflection. The teacher has the chance to act more as a facilitator than as a figure of authority.

THE ROLE OF THE FACILITATOR

As the leader of the class the teacher has the role of facilitator. In this role the teacher's emphasis is on bringing out the participants' experiences and reflections rather than the teacher's answers. The facilitator needs to establish a sense of safety, encourage participation and lead the process of the workshop.

The teacher should focus on positive communication and engaging the participants to take an active part in the workshop. All members of the circle are equally important and share the responsibility for making all participants feel comfortable. The teacher as a facilitator sits in the circle and his or her task is to lead the circle process. It is important that the facilitator spend time on activities that contribute to an inclusive atmosphere where every participant is seen and heard. The facilitator must demonstrate confidence and let every participant speak without being interrupted, or given comments or corrections, but it is the group as such that shares the responsibility of creating an inclusive atmosphere.

The facilitator has the important role of modelling and securing that everyone in the group feels safe, and setting a respectful tone.

Kay Pranis (2005) is an experienced facilitator and sums up the role of the facilitator as follows:

- To create a safe and respectful atmosphere.

- To create a tone that contributes to constructive work and solutions.

- To lead the process according to core values.

- To take a hold of the positive that happens and make clear unsolved problems.

- To be a participant in the community.

THE STRUCTURE OF A RESTORATIVE CIRCLE

We often receive a lot of questions about how we conduct a circle gathering. Questions that are often asked are: 'Is it not a bit awkward to sit face to face in a circle?' 'Can it not easily become a conversation between the teacher and the talkative students?' The answer to these questions is simply: When facilitating a restorative circle you need a fixed structure and we will present how you can build a structure to accommodate the goal of including and motivating all the participants equally. The structure is the same regardless of which grade level you are working with and regardless of the main topic of the circle. We have many years of experience with using circles in an educational context and we will describe how this can be done.

A restorative circle is described through active participation, dialogue and practical activities, role plays, games and reflection. A restorative circle workshop should have a set of structured elements:

- a unifying starter and introduction

- an ice breaker

- a main part

- evaluation

- a unifying closing.

Here is what these different elements of a workshop include:

Outline
Quickly go through the agenda of the meeting, written on a blackboard, flip chart or on a poster. The agenda helps students stay focused.

Check-in
Start by doing a round. All participants say something one at a time – go with the sun (clockwise) – about a theme that is easy for everyone to say something about, for instance: 'Something I need to work on today is…', 'One thing I appreciate about this class is…'. It is alright if someone says 'pass', but they should be given the opportunity to say something when the round is finished.

A 'check-in' engages everyone to participate and gives everyone the chance to be seen and heard.

Game/ice breaker

Use games and activities to create positive energy and laughter. A game serves the purpose of a social mixer.

Main activity

A main activity means using practical activities and training situations connected to the topic, which gives the participants the chance to learn by doing, through experience and reflection. The topic could be 'improved communication', 'class environment', 'planning a social event', 'how to be a good friend', 'conflict', etc.

Summing up and evaluating

What kinds of questions for reflection are relevant when an activity is finished? What is the purpose of the questions for reflection? A moment of reflection should give participants the opportunity to share thoughts and see connections between what has been experienced in the activity and in real life, in class and in life in general. Here are three questions that participants can be asked:

- What happened in this activity?

- How did you find this activity?

- Can you use some of the activities in your own everyday life?

One tip is to use questions that are open for reflection and to omit questions starting with 'why'. It is not always easy to know why things happen or why they are the way they are, and questions on why things are so may be perceived as being accusations.

Check-out

A check-out is an easy activity that strengthens the bonds of the community members, for instance, giving everyone a 'high five'.

The structured facilitating of a circle makes the participants feel they matter and that they are important to the group. In a circle, participants communicate and interact in a way that rarely happens outside the circle. The perspectives, the facts and the stories that are shared in the circle contribute to improved social competence, empathy and positive behaviour.

TALKING PIECE

A beanbag or a small, soft ball can serve the purpose of being a 'talking piece' to be passed from one person to the next in the circle. The person who has the talking piece has the right to speak. This will put stronger focus on the person speaking and it helps the others to be better listeners. The talking piece is a visual sign that they all have a possibility and a responsibility for participating in the process. This may sound idealised, but our experience is that the talking piece has a strange, almost magical power when used in the circle. It disciplines the participants, and there are hardly any disturbances in the workshop, something that is often pointed out as being very positive by the participants.

THE BACKGROUND OF PROBLEM-SOLVING CIRCLES

Proactive and reactive use of restorative circles is rooted in *restorative justice*, which originated in Australia and Canada. This book aims to integrate restorative principle and practice into everyday life at school. The first projects in restorative justice were developed late in the 1970s in Canada and North America as alternatives to traditional criminal law and its punitive system. Since that time restorative justice has spread to many countries including Norway, where the law for mediation services (Lovdata, 1991) is equal in weight to the Norwegian penal code. Restorative justice is implemented in the Council of Mediation and in the Norwegian judicial system, and is used as a supplement or alternative to traditional legal sanctions.

Children as young as 13–14 years old commit crimes but what should society's response be to these children who are also students? In 2014, a type of sanction for young offenders, 'youth penalty', was implemented as an alternative to legal sanctions in order to avoid children being imprisoned.

Youth penalty is typically aimed at young offenders of 15–18 years old who have committed serious crimes or are repeat offenders. Young offenders have different needs to adult offenders and imprisonment not provide any help for young adults breaking the law. The central idea is to help these young adults out of criminal activity, as all experience proves that imprisonment is not suitable for teens or young adults. Schools must participate in the restorative processes of resocialising the youth offender. In order to aid with this, schools need competence in the field of restorative practices.

Youth penalty is handled by the mediation services and is based on restorative processes. The young offenders must participate in a process where all affected parties and representatives from school, social services, the police and criminal welfare are present. To reduce the danger of relapse into criminal activity there is emphasis on early intervention, strict controls and monitoring the young adults in addition to other precautionary activities.

Restorative justice, as an alternative to criminal law, shows promising results, both when it comes to solving conflicts and in health work in general. This approach has over the years been adapted to school settings, proactively and reactively.

In short one can say that circles and restorative practices focus both on building relationships and repairing harm. The affected parties involved listen to each other's stories, experiences and needs, and resolve the matter as democratic citizens and by dialogue (Zehr, 2002).

TWO PARADIGMS

Traditionally, wrongdoing in school is sanctioned by measures such as detention, suspension or expulsion, where the main focus is to find the guilty party and a teacher or the head teacher decides on a sanction. For decades however, schools in many countries have implemented and adapted the use of restorative problem-solving circles as a way of dealing with misbehaviour and violation of school rules. We therefore present Table 1, which demonstrates the differences between the traditional way of thinking and the restorative focus of repairing interpersonal relationships and harm, where the central obligation is to put right the wrongs, based on a restorative approach.

In Part 3 you can read about a case that describes how the restorative approach is used in a bullying situation.

Table 1: Two paradigms

Traditional authority	Alternative authority Restorative justice
• What school rule has been violated?	• Violation of relations or person(s)
• Who is guilty? • Why did he/she do it?	• Who has been hurt/violated? What needs does the hurt person have?
• Focus on the past • A teacher/the head teacher decides on sentence and verdict	• Focus on the future, needs and emotions • Who is obligated to put things in order again?
• Justice is achieved when the school decides on guilt and the appropriate sanctions	• Justice is achieved by the parties involved in the conflict and the school collaborating in order to 'repair the harm'

Source: Model adapted from Zehr, 2002

Table 1 gives an outline of the differences between the two paradigms. The traditional paradigm is to find the guilty party, and give a verdict and a punishment in accordance with the school's regulations. The alternative paradigm shows how schools deal with the breaking of rules based on the principles of restorative justice and with the main focus on the victim's emotions, needs and the future. The parties in a case need support from the school in order to put things right again.

NONVIOLENT COMMUNICATION

Nonviolent Communication is an important communication strategy within the field of restorative practices.

Imagine your actions and behaviour being met with understanding and not scolding, and your teacher talking with you and not to you. Imagine developing self-confidence and self-awareness and feeling safe instead of agitated, with doubts and frustrations that lead to bad choices and less appropriate actions. Classic conflicts contain hurt feelings, accusations and complaints. There is a victim and an offender. There can be physical and emotional violations and sometimes violence. The solution often comes down to finding the guilty party; to determine who is right and who is wrong, who is the hero and who is the villain. Whether conflicts or bullying take place in the home, at school or at work, traditional proactive actions for preventing conflicts are all about pointing the finger at someone, making rules, finding the guilty party and punishing him or her.

In our view this way of thinking just scratches the surface and really does not solve anything. On the contrary, sometimes it only contributes to the conflict continuing and involving more parties. And worse, it contributes to creating divides between people, when it is contact and the sense of belonging to the community that we want, along with a good psychosocial learning environment, one that contributes to personal development and effective learning. Is there another way?

We suggest that all schools receive training in Nonviolent Communication, developed by the American psychologist and conflict mediator, Marshall B. Rosenberg (2003), over 40 years of practice. This is a form of communication and way of being that creates contact and understanding between people, regardless of ethnicity, gender, age, nationality and religious beliefs.

The giraffe and the jackal

Nonviolent Communication is a key activity in our work with dialogue circles and is one of the main activities in Safe Learning's national training course in conflict resolution and restorative practices.

We have all been in situations where we feel we are being totally misunderstood and everything has gone wrong. We leave such situations with a bad feeling, often angry and wondering what actually happened. We wonder what went wrong – and why? What is better than talking directly to the others in order to find out?

This is where Nonviolent Communication comes in. Nonviolent Communication is acknowledged worldwide as a tool for conflict resolution and for enhancing communication – in conflict areas, in prisons, between groups and rival gangs, in work places, between partners in a marriage – and its use is growing in schools all over the world. Nonviolent Communication is also called 'giraffe language'. It is accepting, empathic and is a way of interacting with others without aggression, criticism, judgement or interpretations. Rosenberg uses the images of *giraffe and jackal language* when describing this way of communicating, as is explained in the example below.

With its big heart, the giraffe is empathic, and with its long neck it has a good overview of the situation. It listens for needs with its big ears and is used as a symbol of what Rosenberg labels Nonviolent Communication.

The jackal is a small animal. It sees a little but guesses and interprets the rest. The jackal does not feel safe; it barks and attacks – something that escalates conflicts.

An underlying idea is that behind every aggression, judgement or criticism there is a person with needs that are not met. If, and when, a person accuses you of something, it is challenging to listen to what unmet needs lie behind the accusations. Rosenberg emphasises that one should always listen to what the other person's needs are instead of what the person is thinking of you. Use the 'I' formula – not the *you*!

> There are four steps in giraffe language: *What I observe*: You overtake other cars on a bend in the road.
>
> *What I feel*: When you overtake other cars on a bend, I am scared.
>
> *What I need*: I need to feel safe when I am riding with you in your car.
>
> *What I ask you to do*: Can you please not overtake other cars on a bend, but wait till the road is straight?

Avoid: criticism, attacking, judgement and interpretations, and the words, 'why', 'if', 'but'.

What happens if you stop using the 'you' message and start using the 'I' message? Imagine being understood instead of being reproved; learning instead of being taught; and developing self-confidence, self-awareness and a feeling of safety instead of feelings of unrest, doubt and frustration that lead to unproductive actions. Imagine being able to be open, happy and enthusiastic, and contributing to making life as wonderful as possible for our fellow beings and for the people around us, instead of playing the game of 'who is right?' or 'who is out?' When we change the way we talk, and stop talking about right and wrong, punishment and reward, should and must – instead talking about what we need deep inside – we have a language *for life*.

We will now look into how we can pose questions aligned with the thinking of Nonviolent Communication.

RESTORATIVE QUESTIONS

Restorative questions are most often used in problem-solving, however for more than 20 years we have used the questions in our daily interactions with young students. In this way the students get to rehearse sharing thoughts and feelings, and strengthen reflection, building up their senses of positive self-assertiveness and responsibility.

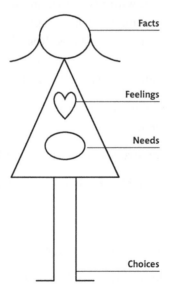

Fig. 6 Listening at different levels

Please keep in mind that it is important to avoid the word 'why' and comments such as 'but you said…' and 'because…'. This is to avoid the offender taking a defensive stance, as such questions and comments may be felt as an accusation. If you ask 'why', the parties may quickly end up in a verbal fight, and thereby the conflict may go into lockdown, preventing you from moving on and resolving the issue.

The usual reaction to a conflict or violation is to let it lie or to get away from the situation. But what happens with the sparks in a fire that is not put out? We know that just one spark may set the whole situation on fire and more people will be involved. Students we interviewed say that conflicts that are not resolved are the reason why they don't come to school.

> I felt so bad I nearly dropped out. At home they thought I was sick. But I was afraid of what the other boys would do to me. I could not take any more shit and threats from them.

> *Boy, 15*

Did no-one in school know what was going on with these boys? Could it be that someone knew, but was reluctant and a bit afraid of getting involved and dealing with it? Or did not have the time to take action? There can be many and complex reasons for why nobody has intervened in a situation.

Restorative communication with people is based on people's ability to act according to logic, emotions and needs, and to make choices. In a school setting all these elements must be embraced and have the best possible conditions so that learning can take place.

The goal is for all students to have a sense of wellbeing and belonging in the group or in school – no-one should feel they are excluded or left out. Adults working with children and young teens need to be aware of how important it is to cater for the basic needs people have: the need for safety, and the need to be seen and acknowledged. Using circles, both proactively and reactively, is well suited for this context and can give the individual a sense of belonging. This may prevent someone from feeling excluded and thereby reduce the subsequent risk of misbehaviour. Many of the young offenders who have committed shootings in schools have been described as loners; people who nobody noticed either in school or in their spare time.

A lot of 'invisible' students skip school and can easily become part of violent conflicts. Here is the story of a boy in 11th grade.

> Not one teacher said my name out loud in class the first semester – I was like 'a nobody', just one that sat in his designated spot in the classroom. I was not stupid, just shy and I needed some help from my teacher, especially in math, but that did not happen. My frustration grew and I skipped school a lot. Then I was called in to the principal and expelled for three days. When I returned, nobody said 'hi' and I felt completely lost. Some days later I just exploded. I felt the teacher ignored me as she only spoke to the nerds in the front row. I burst out of the classroom and screamed and I tore down all the garbage cans in the corridor before I smashed the sink in the toilet. Then someone stopped me. The school reported the incident to the police and, believe it or not, that helped me. I had several meetings with the police and they asked me a lot of good questions and I could speak of everything that was on my mind and how I felt, and then we made an agreement.

> *Boy, 16 – tells his story when talking to the school counsellor*

In a conflict situation the narratives the parties present will be very different. The parties may agree on parts of the incident, but not all. For the parties to tell their whole story in safe surroundings a good tool for communication is needed. This is something we need throughout our lives, so it can be a valuable life skill.

Below are the core questions that are used in restorative communication and meetings. Terry O'Connell, director of Real Justice Australia, is thought of as the pioneer for the development of restorative conferences and restorative questions.

The restorative questions operationalise the five key restorative themes Belinda Hopkins focuses on (Hopkins, 2013):

- unique and equally valued perspectives

- thoughts influence emotions, and emotions influence subsequent actions

- empathy and consideration for others

- identifying needs comes before identifying strategies to meet these needs

- trust and empowerment.

The restorative way of asking questions fosters empathy and shared understanding and gives the parties in a conflict ownership of their own situation.

The facilitator's role is to be a neutral leader of the conversation who asks the questions one after the other so that both parties can communicate what is in their heart, and listen to each other's story.

- What happened?

    - Both parties tell their story, one at a time. Tip: Think carefully through who should talk first. It could be smart to let the person who is most emotionally engaged talk first.

    - To correct any misunderstandings and underline important parts, sum up along the way what the parties are saying.

    - Remember: Never ask 'why'. It can be felt as an attack, and the parties can easily go into defensive mode. It is not easy to know why things happen sometimes.

    - Ask a lot of questions for clarification, so that all details from both sides are presented.

    - It could be necessary to help the parties to limit the conflict.

    - Focus on what the parties agree on.

- What did you think at the time? What do you think now?

    - Pose open, clarifying questions so that as many details as possible are revealed.

- Who is affected by the situation and how?

    - Experience from peer mediation in schools shows that most conflicts in schools happen in classrooms or during recess and, as a consequence, a lot of students are affected by the conflict.

    - Make obvious the parties' views on who is affected by the incident/situation, and how they are affected.

- Talk about emotions. How do you feel about what has happened?

- Conflicts and violations involve emotions, including anger and sadness. The facilitator must try to make the parties talk about their emotions.

- How did you feel when it happened? Can you say something about how you feel now?

- Try to have the parties see the point from the other party's perspective. 'If you had/were…'

- Avoid focusing on guilt. The parties can tend to say things like 'It was him/her that started it'.

- What did you think when it happened? What do you think now that it has happened?

• Talk about needs. What do you need to feel better? What do you need to make things right again?

- What do you need to feel better?

- What is necessary for this never to happen again?

- What do you need to do in order to repair the harm?

• Talk about solutions. What do you want the outcome of this conversation to be?

- What can you do to prevent this from ever happening again?

- What do you think would be smart to do now for the two of you to go on from here?

- What would you suggest?

The facilitator sums up the wishes of the parties. If you have received many suggestions you can write them on a blackboard or on a piece of paper, and the parties can agree to what are the main points.

In Part 2 we give some examples of how circles and restorative practices can be implemented in different settings in schools.

Part 2

Implementing the
Circle Method

Circles can be used at different levels of an organisation: universally (a whole-school approach), selectively (group level) and at an indicated level (individual). Implementation of the method can be done at all levels, on two levels or on one level only. The school will have to decide what is best according to its needs and resources. We recommend starting out on a small scale, gaining experience and gradually implementing the use of circles throughout the organisation.

Interview

An upper secondary school head teacher says this about the use of circles:

> We have undertaken a systematic evaluation of the students' learning environment through our own surveys and later through the national student survey of the students' learning environment for many years. The school has through several years had focus on creating a socially inclusive learning environment. When we were introduced to the use of circles and school mediation, we saw that we could be more systematic in our approach in using the method proactively but also in conflict resolution.
>
> We saw that the use of circles is a good tool for everybody in our school, both for our students and our employees. The use of circles provide the students with 'life skills' as this is a tool they can use in their private lives and in their future professional careers. The systematic training in the use of circles increases a

37

higher relational competency among all members of our school. The implementation of the use of circles develops a greater understanding of the students' learning environment and the employees' working environment.

Starting all visits to our school by sitting in a circle is a nice and efficient way of creating a friendly atmosphere and good meetings with our visitors. As a principal I often demonstrate how we work with the circle method in practice.

When I, or the school's leadership team, want to discuss things with the students – whether it is an ordinary conversation or a conflict resolution with a group of students or a whole class – I/we use circles as the method to make sure that everybody participates or that their opinion in the matter is heard.

I encourage the team leaders in school to use circles in their weekly team meetings in order to make all participants committed to the discussions and to make sure all participants are being heard. All our staff is trained in the use of circles, the latest training taking place during our professional development days this spring (2017). The philosophy and method must be rooted in all staff and students if it is to work as we want it to. We are on our way, but I think we still have a way to go in using the method more thoroughly, also regarding our leadership team.

PLANNING THE IMPLEMENTATION PROCESS

Figure 7 demonstrates the main elements in the implementation process of the use of circles.

When you have decided to start using restorative circles we recommend that you start with 'baby steps'. In other words, start with an activity you as a teacher know and feel comfortable with, and from there gradually expand your repertoire. A good idea may be to make a step-by-step plan for the process, and then reflect on and evaluate the implementation process, making any necessary adjustments.

What does a good school environment look like? What improvements do you want see in your school environment?

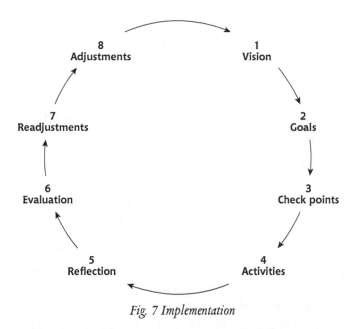

Fig. 7 Implementation

Goal

- All teachers involved committed to the vision, the belief and the practice and with ownership over it.

- Teachers receive training in the use of circles both proactively and reactively.

Activities

- Teachers trained in the use of circles with appropriate activities that can easily be conducted. The focus is on communication and social skills.

- Try out the use of circles in all classes in the grade level every two weeks.

Reflection

Teachers have weekly meetings to reflect on their own practice, share experiences and, if necessary, adjust and improve the content.

Increasingly, the meetings may take the form of using formative assessment in the process of implementing the use of circles.

Evaluation

Set deadlines for evaluations, weekly, monthly and at certain times during the year.

- What are your experiences so far? How have things worked out? Make adjustments and improvements based on experiences in order to adjust the course onwards. Remember to have the students evaluate the circle processes too.

To use circles may seem a bit unfamiliar and awkward for students in 11th grade (16–17 year olds). We recommend the classroom teacher introduces circles when the students express positive and good vibes. Do an activity or a game that makes the students relax and feel safe – safe with each other and safe with the teacher acting as the facilitator. The facilitator should inform the class that the aim of the circle is to get to know each other better and have fun, and also to support each other as individuals and academically.

THE FRAMEWORK FOR RESTORATIVE CIRCLES

The pedagogical background for the activities is based on the socio-constructivist theories of learning, such as of John Dewey and Pablo Freire (Dewey, 1916; Freire, [1968] 1970). 'Learning by doing' and pedagogy for liberation and learning from experience. Thomas Gordon's view on conflicts as a source of positive growth by positive mobilisation of the parties to conquer difficulties and crisis is in harmony with the ideas of a restorative approach, and that the students should be critical co-explorers of the conflict in collaboration with the teacher (Gordon, 1979). The teacher is not only a person who teaches, but also takes on a role as a learner themselves, working with the students in the context reality they know. The aim is to strengthen class culture and increase respect for human values and dignity. Lev Vygotsky's theory (Vygotsky, 1934) points out the importance of the teacher's role as facilitator to allow the student to reach their proximal zone of development. In a collaborative supportive environment, students will exchange thoughts and ideas and thereby serve as (the) more capable peers for each other.

Dewey and Freire shared the understanding that the student should have the experience of meaningful activities and reflection on a deeper level regarding relationships and situations that occur in everyday life.

The purpose of the community-building practices discussed here is to get to know each other better, to build good relationships both among the students in the group and between the teacher and the group, and to create an atmosphere of safety and a sense of unity, and by doing so create a good foundation for reflection and learning. When students know each other well there is less chance of inappropriate or aggressive behaviour and bullying outside of school and on social media.

The community-building practices have been selected so that they will be easy to perform in any classroom. They are meant to be fun and do not require any extra equipment or space. Our experience is that physical activity can ease the tension in a group and create and revive new energy. Several of the games therefore contain elements of movement or physical activity.

The practices can be used to get to know each other and create a sense of safety when the school year starts and during the school year as part of training in collaborative skills and creating group dynamics for building a positive culture for learning in class. There is no right or wrong for what is appropriate to discuss: the teacher should use their professional judgement. Our experience is that no topic is too small or too big in a circle conversation.

A restorative circle is a way of talking with others where:

- all are equal and respected

- all have a chance of talking without being interrupted or receiving negative comments

- all are given a voice

- no participant is more important than any other.

A restorative circle is especially useful:

- when group members need to get to know each other better

- when the group members need to work on and reflect on their class environment

- when the group members disagree on something

- when the group wants to work together as a team

- when the group members wish to share something that is difficult

- when the group members wish to learn from each other.

CREATING AN INCLUSIVE LEARNING COMMUNITY

Interview

A teacher of electronics says this about the use of circles in class:

> One of the most important reasons for using circles is to get to know each other better, to create good relations between the students and listen to each other. We do a check-in with the students every Monday morning and finish the week by sitting in a circle where we evaluate how things went in the course of the week. When the topic is discussed, we use a fuse as a talking piece and each and everyone can talk one at a time. I have very good experiences in using this method. It connects the students and they all have the courage to say something. The circle has a meaning in itself, because everyone can see everyone's faces. To sit in a perfect circle gives us all a good sense of community feeling.

To start or end the school day or week with a circle creates a sense of unity and becomes a ritual for 'where am I now' – in school. All circle members say something, including the teacher. The structure that one person speaks after the other ('Go with the sun', or clockwise), is a set system that gives predictability and helps students to wait, in addition giving everyone some time to think and prepare. 'If the teacher had taken 5 minutes to say something nice or fun, all would be fine', students often say when collaboration is working poorly. We encourage teachers therefore to take 5 minutes to have some fun.

The possibilities are almost endless, but here are some suggestions for topics. Invite people to:

- Have each person introduce themselves not just by name, but by adding an adjective before their name that begins with the same letter as the name. For example, Sweet Saima, Curious Claire, Bold Brian. Have everyone take turns around the circle.

- Name one thing that inspires them to keep on going.

- Identify what they enjoy the most in this class.

- Name a thing the class did well this week.

- Name something they look forward to this week.

- Name a person that has helped them this week.

- Name something they need help with this week.

- What do they need in order to feel at ease in this class?

- Name a thing they like to do in their spare time.

- Name a thing the class can do together.

- Say something nice to the person sitting to your left.

THE QUIET STUDENTS

She just sits there.

Ingrid Lund, 2008

'Still waters run deep', but what course should teachers pursue with the quiet students? This category of student is easily overlooked, and several students that we have interviewed say that the teacher let them be silent, something which has not been to their benefit. There are many reasons why students do not talk, ranging from being shy to being introverted to struggling with anxiety. We who work with children and young adults have a huge responsibility to support and encourage these students to participate in class, and in dialogue workshops, but it must be done with great caution. We should never force anyone to talk, but we should have a thorough plan for oral communication and use a variety of communication methods. Could a dialogue circle be a good way of working for introverted students? Ingrid Lund's research on silent students gives a valuable insight into how these students perceive their school days and how teachers can best facilitate and cater for these students' needs.

Interview

This is what a quiet student (16) says:

> I was the quiet and shy girl in class. I never spoke with anyone in class or in larger groups. Of course I had my ideas and opinions about things too in school, but I never said anything and no-one asked me anything either! My classroom teacher really did not do me any favours in letting me be quiet, I can see that now. Now I dare to speak and answer when the teacher asks a question in class, but I became a different person after I joined the peer mediation scheme. I dare to speak in front of an audience now. I have become really brave. I have got a lot of self-confidence. Now I can even be the host of a seminar! If you never have the courage to participate in discussions, or state your opinion on topics in class, you will somewhat 'disappear', and people will not count you in a way. Then it is easy to lose self-confidence and self-respect. Now, I'm a real talker!

CIRCLE TIME: HAVING FUN – LEARNING TOGETHER

Before starting circle time it is necessary to organise the students' chairs into a circle and then have the students take a seat. When everybody has found their place in the circle, sitting down or standing up, the teacher explains the purpose of sitting in a circle and the rules of how communication will be. It may be a good idea to pose a question for the group regarding a work agreement:

• How should we work together during this lesson?

Suggestions from the students may be: to show each other respect, not utter negative comments, not disturb or interrupt each other. Write down the more important suggestions on the blackboard or on a flip chart and point to this if the students are unruly. Tip: Do not write too many rules: agree on no more than five. It may be an idea for one of the students to do the writing, and for all the students to sign the agreement so that they feel ownership of what they have agreed to. The signed agreement must be put up on the wall and visible.

Work agreement class 11C

❖ Say hello to everyone in the morning

❖ Be helpful

❖ Do not disturb – use indoor voice, work buzz

❖ Collaborate with everyone

❖ Have fun together

Fig. 8 Outline of class work agreement

We emphasise the need for a 'talking piece' – a 'microphone' to regulate the talking. The participants talk one after another and the others listen. This may seem elementary, but think of meetings you participate in and what it feels like to be interrupted, neglected or disturbed by others whispering while you are trying to say something. Very often this situation is one that creates conflicts in a class. The teacher may also be quite annoyed and disturbed in their work as leader of the class.

The teacher may place the students standing up or sitting down in a circle either on a chair or on the floor. If the classroom is too small, it may be necessary to move some desks and chairs in order to make room for a circle. Keep it simple. One alternative is to make use of any empty space inside or outside the classroom. A circle is not always a circle. Be meticulous in that the group makes a geometrical circle, as all participants must be equal in the sense that no-one sits in front and no-one in the back.

Clear instructions will increase the probability of a positive experience and a successful circle. It may prove wise to warm up the participants in the group by 'doing a round' in the circle. One by one the students will hear their own voice and listen to all the others speaking. Check-in and check-out can be used as part of a daily routine to build an active learning environment and create a sense of 'we-feeling'. Warm up activities can be followed by planning and suggestions for work to be done that day or the upcoming week and/or evaluating the work that has been done in the same period.

The possibility to say 'pass'

It is not always that easy to speak on command when put 'on the spot'. We therefore recommend that there is the possibility for the circle participants to say 'pass', and that they are given an opportunity to speak when the (first) round is finished. Consider whether it would be best to alternate between doing a round, going into pairs for dialogue, small groups or 'speaking freely'/open microphone? Let there be a couple of minutes of silence between activities, which can give participants a good opportunity for reflection.

OUTLINE OF THE FIRST CIRCLE TIME

Circle time has a fixed structure:

1. Present the topic of the circle time.

2. Check-in.

3. Games.

4. Today's topic.

5. Evaluation and reflection.

6. Check-out.

Theme: To get to know each other, create a safe atmosphere

Time: 45 minutes

The teacher is part of the circle. The activities are presented in Part 4.

Time	Activity	Purpose	Remember
5 minutes	Hi and welcome! Facilitator/instructor explains briefly what a circle is, and the agenda	Focus and safety	Chairs in a circle Agenda written on a blackboard or a flip chart 'Talking piece'
10 minutes	Check-in! Name a thing you're looking forward to at school this week. Do the round one by one. Everybody will speak and listen to what the others say. Everybody is equal in this activity!	Activate all participants and get to know each other	
10 minutes	Game 'The Sun Shines on…'	Have fun, get to know each other and move about a bit	
15 minutes	Work agreement – choose A or B A 'Four Small Words' (see Part 4) B Pair work, reflect together for two minutes. Every pair agrees on two things that are important for a good working relationship, and shares this with the others. The facilitator writes the suggestions on the wall or on the flip chart, etc. Group discussion. The class agrees on five rules that are written on a poster visible to everyone	Practise communication Create a safe atmosphere and a clear structure	Flip chart or a blackboard Big sheet of paper/poster
5 minutes	Check-out! Do the round Each participant names an activity they enjoyed today Positive feedback	Build community Create a sense of unity	

RESTORATIVE CIRCLES AS A DAILY ROUTINE

There are many schools in Norway and other countries that practise the use of circles as a means of building strong and inclusive learning environments and to encourage student participation. Circle time is used in different ways: some schools use circle time on Monday morning as a start to the week and on Friday afternoons to close the week. In some other schools the classes use circle time once every other week, and other schools may choose to give all classes eight hours of training (90 minutes × 4) in restorative conflict resolution. When this work is successful, it will promote good psychosocial health, diminish the growth of negative behaviour, exclusion and bullying, and reduce the incidence of conflicts, violence, racism and students being subject to radicalisation.

Interview

A PSE (personal and social education) teacher says it like this:

> Training staff in the use of circles and restorative practices does not need to take a lot of time. In our school we have a long experience in working with student mediation, and some teachers have been through the basic training in student mediation, but there is a need for refresher and a run-through of new, practical activities that all teachers need in their everyday pedagogical work. The social teacher and the resource teacher for mediation are frequently given 15 minutes of the teachers' weekly planning time to run through practical activities based on situations or incidents the teachers report have happened in the class or during recess. That way the use of circles becomes part of all the staff's common ground and part of the school routine.

In the spring of 2014 two schools in Oslo received financial support from the Directorate for Education and Training. Both schools got funding to develop the use of restorative circles in order to improve the learning environment. The primary school named these circle meetings 'environment meetings' and they took place at every grade level every two weeks. The upper secondary school used their funding to implement the use of circles in year one (year 11 in UK or grade 11 in the US). This school used the term 'dialogue workshop', focusing on specific topics of learning such as conflict analysis, Nonviolent Communication and community-building. The first dialogue workshop was mandatory at the beginning of the school year, and the other took place after the student survey was conducted at the beginning of November. The third dialogue workshop took place when there were conflicts that had affected the learning environment negatively. In the spring of 2016 two Master's dissertations were written about these projects (Halstensen, 2016; Karlsen, 2016). The use of environment meetings and dialogue workshops spread quickly in Norwegian primary and secondary schools. In the next section we will have a closer look at the dialogue workshop.

OUTLINE OF A DIALOGUE WORKSHOP

The term 'dialogue workshop' is used when the focus is on specific learning goals.

Theme: Safety and wellbeing. Conflict analysis – 'giraffe versus jackal language'

The classroom teacher participates in the circle

Time: 90 minutes

The activity is described in Part 4.

Time	Activity	Purpose	Remember
5 minutes	Hi and welcome! Presentation of: • background and purpose of the dialogue workshop • plan • the facilitator (if that is another teacher)	Concentration and predictability	Chairs in a circle Talking piece Written agenda on blackboard or flip chart Facilitator welcomes the participants and presents the agenda

cont.

Time	Activity	Purpose	Remember
10 minutes	Check-in 30 seconds: reflection Name and things I like to do/don't like to do in my spare time Reflection	Engage all participants Get to know each other	Do the round – one by one – with the sun
10 minutes	Game: 'The Sun Shines on…'	Humour and physical activity	Share something about yourself Get to know each other
15 minutes	Pair/dialogue One question for interview: Name two things you are good at The pairs take turns in presenting the other to the group by saying what the other person says he or she is good at What thoughts came to your mind just now? Reflection: Were you represented correctly?	Rehearse dialogue – Competency Rehearse active listening	
15 minutes	Conflict In pairs: Minor conflicts in class Volunteers share Reflection in group Introduction of the 'conflict staircase'	Awareness and reflection on conflicts and their impact on the learning environment	Poster 'conflict staircase'
15 minutes	Introduce giraffe language 'I' and 'you' messages Activity: 'Giraffe–Jackal'	Rehearse positive communication	Noniolent Communication Poster: 'giraffe language' The steps in Nonviolent Communication

10 minutes	'Paper – Not Floor' In groups of four Reflection	Rehearse collaboration Creativity, have fun	Activities in groups on the floor Big sheets of paper
10 minutes	Assessment An activity I liked/did not like How well do you think the class worked this hour – on a scale from 1 to 10?	Rehearse assessment	Standing circle
1 minute	Check-out! Texas Hug	Build community	'We' One community

PEER EDUCATION

Young adults often make their choices based on what their peers or role models do rather than on what they know and what is best for them. Peer educators can communicate and relate to other young adults in a way that grown ups cannot. So why not educate peers to help their fellow young adults make good choices?

Over the past 20 years many schools have worked on developing peer education. One way of doing it is to train the student council members in the use of circles. We have experienced that training the student council members in the use of circles and circle activities has a positive effect on the learning environment. Student council members are often elected because they are popular among their fellow students and they signed up for the election because they want to serve the class or school community. The training we have provided is a basic training that includes giraffe versus jackal language, conflict escalation and conflict resolution, and the five restorative questions. The peer educators work alongside the teacher and can run activities in class or whole-school activities and, in this way, be good supporters for both students and teachers.

Students interviewed said this about peer education:

'We listen more closely to our peers than to our teachers, and we can be more open and more honest with a peer'.

'It is better to talk to our class representative as he or she understands me, more so than an adult'.

In short, we can sum it up like this:

- Peers have skills adults do not possess, because they are young.

- Peers are equal to their classmates, so there is no power imbalance.

- Peers speak the same language, use the same jargon, etc. as their classmates.

- Peers know the adolescent culture.

- Peers understand peers.

- Peers are positive role models and have an impact on their peers.

Being young adults peer educators can relate to their fellow students in a different way from grown ups. It is easier for the young adults to understand each other than for an adult. And, as the students claim, it is easier to be open and speak freely to someone who is your own age. A peer educator can be a friend who listens to his or her peer(s) and interacts with them if there are things that need to be addressed. A peer educator can help out with information or inspire and empower others to move forward in their lives. A peer educator can lead topics of discussions in a circle time, provide materials for and create awareness of topics that are of interest, and help plan fun events for the group. A peer educator can challenge unhealthy attitudes and behaviour, correct misperceptions about social norms, confront language or activities that are abusive or insulting and, by doing so, be a good role model to their peers. Peer educators can be good team members by being positive and speaking positively about others, and supporting the teachers and all the stakeholders in the school community.

CIRCLE TIME USED IN TUTOR GROUPS

Participating in a restorative circle is a great way to rehearse responsibility and let your voice be heard. In this way student participation and understanding of democracy will be strengthened. Tutor groups are a good forum for discussing topics related to class and to school. What is a good classroom friend? What can we do to eliminate tardiness? How can we make our learning environment the best possible? How can we create a good school? What is a good school? Tutor groups are a place where the teacher and students focus on collaboration and being good classmates and how to create a good learning environment, and where grades and assessments are not the main focus.

If the school has chosen to put circle time on the schedule, we believe there is a need to show how to do it: a model or a guideline for the teachers. Tutor groups are a splendid opportunity to get to know each other, learn from each other and give the students a chance to discuss and reflect on whether they enjoy the class or not. Students say that if they know each other well, they are far less likely to bully each other or send/post negative or hurtful messages on the net.

OUTLINE OF THE USE OF CIRCLE TIME IN TUTOR GROUPS

Time	Activity	How	Purpose
5 minutes	Put chairs in a circle. Agenda written on the blackboard or a flip chart	Students and teacher all sit in a circle. Make sure the circle is a complete mathematical circle and work with the sun	Symbolise unity/ community, create a good working environment
5 minutes	Hi and welcome! Present today's agenda		Common focus
10 minutes	Check-in • name and how I am today • a secret talent that I have	Do the round, one by one, twice	All get to say something, be heard be 'equal'
10 minutes	'The Sun Shines on…' Or 'Paper – Not Floor'	Warm up game	Physical activity and laughter

cont.

Time	Activity	How	Purpose
10 minutes	Complete the sentence... I feel respected when... I feel I am not respected when...	Pair activity Ask for a volunteer: Can someone share their thoughts with the group? Reflection: How does this impact the community/the class environment?	Reflection
5 minutes	'Hurricane'	Teacher says the word 'hurricane', and all participants find a new seat in the circle, and a new partner	Get to know other classmates better, and not their regular friends/peers
10 minutes	Class environment • one strength • one challenge	Pair work Notes on the blackboard/ flip chart; the colour green for strengths and the colour red for challenges	Reflection
10 minutes	1 Who is responsible for the class environment? 2 What can you do to improve the class environment?	Do the round	Reflection and evaluation
5 minutes	Assessment/ evaluation • one thought I take with me • one thing I did well today	Standing circle. Do the round twice	Practise assessment/ evaluation
1 minutes	Closing the circle - Texas Hug	All participants in a standing circle, arms on each others' shoulders, on command take a step back and two long steps forward and shout: 'Yeah!'	Build community

FOSTERING WELLBEING WHILE WORKING ON ACADEMIC SUBJECTS

Wellbeing and learning are closely interconnected. Students who thrive in school also perform well academically. Research shows a close connection between students' social skills and their academic achievements (Hattie, 2008). Social skills and attitudes are fostered in every class and hour in school, not only in primary school but also in secondary and upper secondary school, and it is a life-long process. There are many ways to give instructions, but which one helps students to remember the best? Research done by Bethel (https://www.fitnyc.edu/files/pdfs/CET_Pyramid.pdf) shows that methods of passive instruction such as lectures are the least beneficial, and practical training with instruction is the best. Which method is most widely used in educational systems?

In kindergarten there is a tradition of gathering the children for 'circle time'. The children sit in a circle. The structure is not as fixed as is described earlier, but the activity can be to sing a song, play a game and talk about feelings and things that make the children happy. It is a good strategy that engages all the children in a fun way.

How can we structure the work in class so that all the students are engaged and equal and motivated to take responsibility and participate in the activities? How can the teacher build good relations with the class and with each individual student through communication so that they thrive and reach their academic potential?

When students work in a circle, they can work individually, together in pairs or in groups. The students learn from each other; they become engaged and speak up without being afraid of being ridiculed by others. It is a good idea to start with small, easy tasks and expand gradually from there. One factor to take into consideration is of course the attention span of the students and how long they are capable of staying on task. And remember to vary tasks and ways of working as that motivates the students.

Having the students work when sitting in a circle ensures that every student is actively engaged in the work, something that, again, will enhance the learning outcome. Since some of the students may feel it is a bit scary to work this way the first time, it is important to give clear instructions for what is going to happen and why. The rule is that ridicule is not allowed and that the way of working is for everyone to improve their skills.

The teacher organises the work so that the students will work with a new partner for a certain length of time. By doing so the teacher ensures that all students are active and that they will have worked with everyone in the class, and again this provide opportunities for the students to improve their social skills, which helps build a safe and inclusive learning environment and leads them to become more responsible and caring, competent and autonomous citizens.

We are inspired by Belinda Hopkins and her great work using restorative approaches in schools – also with a focus on the teachers' role and daily academic work with the students. Hopkins encourages teachers to rethink their role as authority in the classroom and develop the qualities of humility and curiosity, to act restoratively. She suggests the restorative teacher interacts using phrases like the following:

- I don't know, what do you think?

- What's happening here?

- Interesting, tell me how you arrived at that idea?

- Go on, I'm curious. Tell me more.

(Hopkins, 2011, p. 181)

Hopkins maintains that a lot of young people's misbehaviour is simply a response to a curriculum and a system they find irrelevant and boring. There is evidence to support the conclusion that when behavioural problems increase in classrooms, one of the first factors to be examined should be instructional procedures and materials and their appropriateness for the offending student (Hopkins et al., 2011, p. 184).

However, 'the blame on you' approach and traditional sanctions and punishments are the most common responses to students' misbehaviour. In our experience, these forms of discipline based on power, control and compliance can easily lead to anger and negative relationships. And the young person learns only to a limited extent how to settle disputes or conflicts. The teacher is the most significant factor that can result in effective learning – and the relationship between teacher and student is crucial for good academic results and for both students' and teachers' wellbeing.

There seems to be a need for change, a transformation of the classroom climate from, for the most part, being based on authoritarian power and control, to being a restorative classroom. Implementing the values and principles as described in Part 1 is no quick fix. Changes take time, several years, and must be systematic in one class, or grade level, or as a whole-school approach if they are to be effective both socially and academically.

So, there is no point in waiting: start right away. In the next section we describe how restorative circles can be used in English in grade/year 11 (16 year olds).

OUTLINE OF THE USE OF RESTORATIVE PRACTICES IN ACADEMIC SUBJECTS

The task must be adapted according to the students' age in terms of content and time. To keep up the energy, remember to do an activity, for instance 'The Sun Shines on…' with a theme such as colours, colours of something the participants are wearing or their favourite colour, hobbies, etc.

Subject: English

Topic: Oral English – Communication, title: 'My career'

Purpose: This is the initial phase of a project where the students are to look into different careers they may like to pursue. What type of training is required? Would they need to go to college? How long a study is it? What are the requirements to get in? How many study places are available? At a later stage they will interview one person working in their chosen profession.

Grade: 11

Time: 70 minutes

The activities are presented in Part 4.

Time	What	Purpose	Remember
5 minutes	Hi and welcome! The teacher presents the agenda (the agenda is written on the blackboard)	Create a friendly atmosphere and spur motivation	Chairs placed in a circle, 'talking piece'
5 minutes	Check-in! Do the round – name and answer: How did you get to school today?	Warm up before the tasks Everyone's voice is heard, and everyone listens to one another	
5 minutes	Game 'Hurricane'	Laugh and have fun	
5 minutes	The teacher poses questions to the class: Who is your idol, or role model? Why is this person your role model? What sources or facts do you base your opinion on?	Students practice working in pairs, posing questions and answering them Present your answers to your peer	Decide who is working together in pairs
15 minutes	Main activity – choose two texts on two different professions and read the text to your partner	Practise the words, practise dialogue, Look at vocabulary	Write the words on the blackboard Ask students to write down new words
20 minutes	Answer the questions related to your chosen profession, present questions and your answers to your partner Work on presenting your profession and give reasons for why you chose the profession	Rehearse oral presentations	

10 minutes	Present your chosen profession in groups of four	Practise speaking in front of others	The other students in the group give feedback
5 minutes	Summing up the first lesson Do the round in the circle What did you learn today?	Students practise speaking their mind	Name one thing you learnt today? What do you think the class learnt today?
	Check-out! Texas Hug	Build community	

Part 3

Restoring Relations

Problem-solving circles can be effective in cases with two parties, groups and in a class regardless of the age group and the severity of the incident. Schools using restorative approaches in handling conflicts and actions of misbehaviour notice a positive effect on the whole school community.

SCHOOLS – ARENAS FOR SOCIALISATION

Social skills are basic skills for children and young adults allowing them to interact and participate in a social reality in all social settings. How can school help students develop social skills, such as self-esteem and empowerment? Research strongly indicates that health and education are intertwined. A good learning environment promotes learning and students' wellbeing. And Hattie says that good working relations and inclusive learning environments are cornerstones of all pedagogical activity (2012).

Working relations and feelings of safety grow from interaction between teens in a group and between the group and the teacher. Good classroom management and a positive social class environment pave the ground for good academic results. The teacher's role as classroom manager is the single most important factor for creating motivation and high academic scores (Hattie, 2012). When teachers demonstrate good classroom management, all students look forward to their school day, and so does the teacher.

VIOLENCE, NOISE AND UNREST

In many classrooms teachers and students witness unruly behaviour, noise, disciplinary problems, conflicts and bullying. The PISA Survey 2015 reports that students think there is too much noise in their classes and that teachers spend a lot of time quietening the students so that the lesson can begin. According to the Student Survey Norway (Elevundersøkelsen, 2015) 3.7 per cent of the students surveyed reported bullying, and 14.7 per cent of the students had experienced teasing, exclusion, gossiping, threats, negative comments about their looks and physical abuse such as punches, pushing and kicking.

Every day thousands of children and teens are exposed to violating comments and behaviour. It would appear as if the school's traditional instruments for creating a good working environment do not always provide the expected results. Violation of rules is handled differently in schools depending on the age of the child and the severity of the violation. By using the traditional authority paradigm, whereby disruptive behaviour will only be handled as a violation of rules by allocation of guilt and punishment, the outcome can be contrary to what is desired. Schools should work systematically at all levels of the school environment in order to prevent bullying (O'Moore, 2010).

A student of 15 put it this way:

> The way parents solve conflicts with kids – by scolding and yelling – does not work, at least not in the long run / not for long. This does not work in schools either when the teacher yells and scolds you in class, and makes you leave the classroom and tells you to wait in the hallway. You feel you are being denounced and subjected to unfair treatment and it just makes you feel even more angry.

THE BYSTANDER EFFECT

The bystander, onlooker effect is a social psychological phenomenon in which individuals are less likely to offer help to a victim when other people are present. The greater number of bystanders, onlookers the less likely it is that anyone of them will help. The bystander, onlooker effect is strong. In school text this is highly relevant in cases of bullying when a lot of onlookers see that a student is being bullied, but do not intervene.

HOW DOES THIS RELATE TO THE CLASSROOM?

As teachers we can often experience that the class will protect the rebellious young person. Even if classmates are tired of noise and unruly behaviour from their peer they will almost always support them against the teacher. Students group up with each other for the most part – and not with the teacher. As a result, the community of students will not benefit from the punishment given to the young rebel. Yelling, scolding, suspension and expulsion do not seem to have the intended effect. The bystander effect is strong. How can the teacher get the young adults on his side instead of as his opponents?

In accordance with government policies in many countries social skills should permeate the traditional curriculum. In order to develop the students' social skills schools must facilitate instruction so that the students can practise interaction, collaboration and conflict resolution. Their education must contribute to social connection and mastering of different roles in society, working life and spare time. Reports and surveys such as PISA and the Student Survey confirm that traditional sanctions for violation of school rules do not work as expected.

Teachers say they need more tools that promote students' social skills. There are a number of organisations that can provide schools with training based on restorative circles; for example, Safe Learning (Norway), Transforming Conflict (UK) and the International Institute for Restorative Practices (USA).

HOW TO CHANGE MISBEHAVIOUR IN CLASS

How can schools start to change the negative climate in classes where there are many conflicts? It is very often that conflicts start with a minor incident, contrasting views or a disagreement that the parties cannot solve by themselves. Conflicts that are not dealt with will rapidly escalate and grow into a bigger conflict and more people will become involved. As a result, a conflict that is not solved will spur other conflicts. Minor incidents in the classroom or the school yard may easily lead to conflict escalation.

CONFLICT ESCALATION

Minor incidents may easily lead to bigger conflicts and can be severe if not dealt with. Lederach's (2005) model of conflict escalation is as follows: A conflict may start with a minor disagreement, then moves on to personal attack and blaming each other for being responsible or for having said or done things that are unfavourable to the other. The problem escalates and communication stops. The situation escalates and those involved split into two parties who are 'enemies'; the two parties dig into their trenches and they are separated.

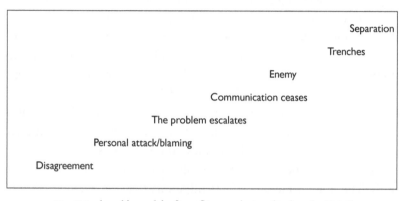

Fig. 9 Lederach's model of conflict escalation (Lederach, 2005)

All conflicts have the same pattern of development regardless of whether they are between two parties, between groups or between countries. Students, like all people, will experience conflicts in their lives. The way schools deal with conflicts will model how students learn to deal with conflicts in their lives in the future. How can we prevent a conflict from escalating?

Staring, screaming, poor choice of words, body language and intonation may block the ability of the parties to talk about what they really disagree on or are unhappy about and what the root of the unpleasantness is. The original underlying conflict is known as the *root conflict* (Galtung, 2003). Such disruptive behaviours as described are expressions of unmet psychological needs.

Schools have a traditional strategy for handling disruptive behaviour and conflicts, and it seems as if schools continue to use sanctions such as suspension, expulsion and detention. But are these sanctions effective? Schools need a new strategy so the parties involved in conflicts can come together and communicate and listen to each other's perspectives in order to find ways of interacting in the future and learn to be responsible for their own actions. Restorative circles could be the preferred new strategy. Conflicts that are solved in a restorative way can be the turning point and lead to personal development and serve as life skills. The conflicting parties are encouraged to take responsibility for finding solutions they agree on in the future.

CONFLICT AS PROPERTY

The idea is simple in that the decisions are made by those persons that are most affected by a situation or are involved in a case. According to Nils Christie, conflicts are best solved by the persons that are affected and have ownership of the conflict (Christie, 1977). Christie also labelled lawyers 'conflict thieves'; in schools we could perhaps say that the conflict thieves are teachers and school leaders. The circle method and restorative practices emphasise the need to encourage students and staff to take a greater responsibility for the community, to develop good relationships and restore/repair the community when things go wrong.

Reports from the USA show that schools that use restorative practices improve students' learning outcomes, and the students take on more responsibility both in school and in the outside world. One example is in the state of Maine, where 14 schools are participating in a five-year-long project that started in 2014 (www.restorativeworks.net).

Let us see how a conflict was solved in a class with 30 students where there had been a lot of noise for a long period of time.

CASE
Class Affected By Misbehaviour

Backdrop

> Over a long period of time there had been a lot of noise and unrest in the class of 30 students, and there had been several incidents of truancy, exclusion, bullying and violations of school

rules. The situation was at a standstill and chaotic. Students were complaining about the teachers and the teachers were complaining about the students. Several students were at risk of failing courses and having their conduct grades lowered. Both teachers and students had sent the school written reports and complaints, and councillors and heads of department had had several serious talks with the students, but nothing seemed to help. How did the school respond to this? The traditional sanctions did not work, and there was a need for a major change that would include all parties and stakeholders. The school's leadership team turned to the school mediators and together they came up with a plan of doing a restorative circle in class with all the students and the teachers. A school mediator is an adult well trained in the field of restorative practices, and is a certified facilitator of restorative circles. Very often the school councillor or social teacher serves as the school mediator.

Preparatory meetings with some students and teachers were held prior to the circle.

The purpose of these meetings was to map the problems, ensure that all voices were heard and articulate their needs for a better learning environment. The main questions in these individual preparatory meetings were:

- What is happening in class?

- What are your thoughts on what is happening?

- How do you feel about the situation in class?

- Who is responsible for putting things right?

- What can you do to help?

If the negative vibes or unpleasant incidents were mentioned, they asked:

- What has your own contribution been to the negative vibes in the class?

- What has your contribution been to the unpleasant incidents?

Here is a short description of how the process was done, and the activities that were conducted in class with 27 participants. The meeting lasted 90 minutes. The structure of the meeting was written on the blackboard, and the participants were sitting on chairs placed in a circle. The activities that were used are described in Part 4.

In order to facilitate a restorative meeting like this you need to have experience as facilitator. Two facilitators to are needed to lead the meeting, and then to debrief the meeting afterwards. The most important thing is to prepare well and conduct individual meetings with the teacher, the class representative and a significant few others who have been involved in negative incidents.

The restorative circle was conducted in the following way:

Check-in: We did the round one by one with the sun. Each person said their name and one thing they thought was positive about the class. A big heart was drawn on the blackboard where all the positive words were written, inside the drawing of the heart and in green. The deputy principal wrote a summary of the meeting.

Pair activity, A and B (2 minutes): Tell your partner about two things that you enjoy in class. Present the results in the plenary where A says what B means and vice versa. What is said is written down on the blackboard, written around the heart with a red marker.

Reflection in pairs (2 minutes): How to get more of the positive/ good things to 'grow'? Or how can we reduce or prevent the negative from happening?

After this, anyone could speak, but few wanted to say something, the situation was fragile and not secure.

Open question: Have you contributed to the negative vibes in class? Raise your hand if you wish to answer. The students raised their hands one by one, including the teacher and the head teacher. They took responsibility for their own classroom behaviour.

New open question: What can you do to improve the learning environment? The group came up with a lot of good suggestions.

Reflection in small groups of four: How can we make this happen?

It was obvious that the student body consisted of different social factions of students. The facilitator asked them to reveal the groups and instantly the students were grouped into four groups. The facilitator then asked how to proceed. The students had a lot on their mind, but time was up and the facilitator had to go on with the work in another way. The students came up with the idea of selecting one student from each of the four groups who would meet with a school mediator in a circle. The purpose of the circle was to come up with suggestions for restoring the relationships between the classmates and the teacher. A dialogue circle was scheduled.

- The circle was wrapped up with an evaluation with the participants standing up. One by one the students shared their own thoughts and reflections. Several students said: 'Why have we not done this before?', 'This works, I believe in it, I don't want to distract the teacher. I just want to feel better in class.'

- A 'Texas Hug' closed the meeting with good vibrations in the group (see instructions in Part 4).

The follow-up meeting with the representatives from the four 'factions' was held as agreed to. And the group representatives came up with a plan to present to their classroom teacher and to the class.

The students had a wish to learn more about communication and communication strategies. The class was therefore invited to a workshop with the topic: Nonviolent Communication and different strategies for communication, including the Social Disciplinary Window described in the next section. The outcome of this process was very positive both for the students and for the teacher in this class.

THE SOCIAL DISCIPLINARY WINDOW

To accommodate the students' wishes the workshop was conducted as planned. As previously described we focused on two communication models. Nonviolent Communication is presented in Part 1. The Social Disciplinary Window model presents four basic communication strategies (Wachtel and Costello, 2009). The four communication strategies were presented and reflected upon. The class worked on some cases to see how the language we use can affect a communication situation positively and negatively. The main purpose of this activity was to give the individual students a better understanding of their own role and responsibility when interacting with others using dialogue in a restorative way.

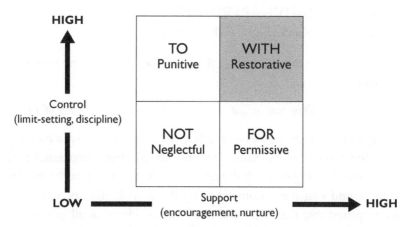

Fig. 10 The Social Disciplinary Window (adapted by Paul McCold and Ted Wachtel) (Castello, B., Wachtel, J. and Wachtel, T. (2010))

The model can be used on many levels, both in communication between two individuals and in communication in groups. If you only use a high degree of control and very little support as the answer to misbehaviour, you have an authoritarian leadership style, talking *to* and giving commands. Those who only respond with a lot of support and a low degree of control often act on behalf of the other party. In reality they are talking on behalf of the other party as they are permissive and excusing. What does the other party learn from this? The answer is obvious: it is okay to do as I do, I will continue to act as usual. If your response has both a low degree of control and a low degree of support, and you ignore the incident or the negative situation, then you are dangerously close to an irresponsible leadership style (although it can be the right response in specific situations. And what does the child/student learn from this? It is okay to do as I do.

To talk *with* entails both a high degree of control and a high degree of support. This authoritative perspective, to talk *with*, enhances dialogue and restorative principles and values. It gives the parties an opportunity to tell their story and the chance to participate and take responsibility for their own choices and contribute further to the process. This approach was, as mentioned above, chosen in the work with the case that is described in the previous paragraph.

CAN RESTORATIVE APPROACHES BE OFFERED IN CASES OF BULLYING?

It doesn't help to say anything, they don't do anything…no matter what.

Odin was bullied in two schools. Odin died at the age of 13.

The quotation above comes from a boy who died tragically in Norway as a direct result of bullying. Parents and children maintained that their concerns regarding bullying were not taken seriously by the schools, and that the actions taken by the schools did not work. We are surprised that the media did not raise the idea that all grown ups must work proactively and systematically over time to develop safe and inclusive environments/adolescence arenas to prevent exclusion and give the young a feeling of belonging.

The term bullying is used for all types of violations big or small. The parties to the unpleasant incident own the experience and, as we see it, any suspicion or concern about bullying should be handled individually. Bullying is a complex social problem that is not only confined to children and young adults – reports have concluded that even adults can be bullied in the workplace (see www.gov.uk/workplace-bullying-and-harrassment; Skåland, 2016).

CASE

Bullying

Restorative circles can be offered in handling cases of bullying as an alternative or supplement to other supportive activities. Knut's case describes how a restorative approach was used.

Knut

Suddenly a student comes running into the office of the school mediator, throws himself on the couch and leans forward with his head in his hands. He starts crying. 'I cannot take any more,' he sobs. He shows the school mediator a swollen fist. Bit by bit the story unfolds as he tells me what has happened. A student in class, 'Ole', had for a long time bothered and bullied him, and time and again had called him a 'loser'. Today he had had it. Anger and despair pressed on. He could not take any more hurtful comments and bullying without doing something. Knut was afraid of hurting others. He had to get away from the offender and the intolerable situation. He ran out of the classroom and hit a brick wall as hard as he could. Knut chose to hurt himself instead of hurting the other student.

Knut described himself as a victim of bullying and stated that he had never said a word to any adults about his situation. He had experienced bullying in secondary school several times and he had found his own way of dealing with the hurtful situations he was facing. Knut was scared, angry and in despair, and he did not want to fight – he just wanted to be left alone. Every time the bullies came, he managed to escape the situation by running away. He found some hard wall or a metal signpost to hit. Today it all went wrong, he broke his hand. For the first time Knut asked an adult for help – the school mediator – whom he had got to know since his class had been given training in mediation. Knut had a lot to talk about and sat for a long time before he went to the nurse, who accompanied him to the emergency room at the hospital to get treatment for his broken hand. His parents were notified and they agreed to meet in the emergency room. It was agreed that Knut would meet in the office of the school mediator the next day after the first class.

The next day, Knut appeared in the doorway with his hand in a cast. The school's leadership team and the counsellor had been notified of the incident and they participated in the meeting. The parents wanted to be briefed about the situation at the end of the day. The main purpose of the meeting was to map out the events of the whole situation, not only the incident the previous day. Knut had only one wish and that was to speak directly to the offender, Ole, without any other students present. He wanted to say how angry he was and desperate he felt and that he wanted to quit school. Knut also wanted to know what Ole had against him and ask that he leave him alone. Knut wanted to return to class after the meeting and he did. A few minutes later a group of students came to ask what had happened. They were clearly upset and touched by the situation, and rumours were spreading about what had happened.

The rest of the day was devoted to meetings and information. First, a plan of action was made about who should do what and in which order. What method should be used? Should the school comply with Knut's request for a face-to-face meeting? Should anyone be expelled? The head of department and the school mediator collaborated on the procedure of the action plan and the necessary formalities were carried out. Ole was willing to meet Knut in a restorative meeting. And then the actual and detailed planning of the process could begin.

Good planning takes time, and in such severe cases as the case of Knut it is very important that all participants in the circle are well prepared. The school leadership team chose to use restorative approaches in the work with this case and mapped out a plan for facilitating the restorative circle with the help of two external facilitators.

> The bullying situation affected a lot of people; the two boys were the most affected of course, but classmates, teachers and parents were also affected. If there were a restorative meeting with many participants it could easily lead to the two boys not feeling safe and possibly not participating or being open and honest, and

others could easily take the lead in the meeting. A restorative meeting is a time-consuming process and all participants should be prepared for this way of meeting and know their role in order to secure a safe environment and a constructive dialogue. To make sure that the two boys felt secure and well prepared for the restorative meeting, the facilitators invited them to individual preparatory meetings. After this, a face-to-face meeting with Knut and Ole took place. They both decided to bring a person for support to the preparatory meeting. Knut chose to bring the school nurse, whom he had had several talks with after the visit to the hospital, and Ole chose to bring the school counsellor. The support persons participated first and foremost to secure a safe atmosphere for both parties in the meeting.

Knut got the chance to tell Ole how he felt, how angry and desperate he had been. There were a lot of emotions and tears in the meeting. Ole said he was sorry and that he understood what Knut was talking about, and he understood the emotions Knut described. He himself had experienced bullying at his previous school. The boys agreed to say hi and talk to each other in ordinary polite terms from now on. Both parties had a wish that the class should be informed about what the two had agreed to.

These were the main points they wanted to put down in the written agreement the two signed after the meeting.

Then the process of preparing the restorative circle began. Who should participate? In addition to the boys who were most affected by the incident the following persons were invited to participate: the parents, a representative from the school's leadership team, the classroom teacher, the counsellor, the school nurse and two classmates. Ten people in all participated in the restorative circle.

The two facilitators worked on the preparations and interviewed all the participants individually to inform them of the purpose of the circle meeting and how the meeting would be conducted.

Participants in the restorative circle

- Knut and Ole (both parties brought their fathers with them)

- classroom teacher

- two class mates

- the school nurse

- the school councillor

- the school principal

- facilitators: two facilitators from the Norwegian Mediation Service.

The facilitators welcomed everyone to the meeting and briefly explained the reason for and the purpose of the meeting and reassured them that everyone would be given the opportunity to speak. Knut spoke first, then the offender. Then the other participants were invited to speak.

Questions asked of the main parties

- What has happened?

- Who has been affected?

- What has been the most difficult?

- What do you need to feel better or put things right again?

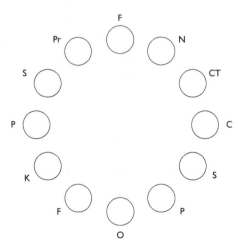

Fig. 11 The participants' places in a restorative meeting
(F– facilitator, K – Knut, O – Ole, P – parent, N – nurse, S – student,
C – counsellor, Pr – principal, CT – classroom teacher)

The meeting lasted nearly 3 hours and a lot of concerns came up. The two students from the class took on the responsibility of assuring the participants that they would keep an eye out and take proper action if there were any signs of name calling in the future. Both were ashamed that they had known what had been going on but had not intervened between the two. Some refreshments were served while the facilitators wrote the agreement down. All the participants in the restorative meeting signed the agreement. A follow-up meeting with the two boys was conducted two weeks after the restorative meeting to ensure that Knut was alright and that the agreement had been kept by both boys.

Both boys participated in a peer mediation course later on.

BULLYING ON SOCIAL MEDIA

Bullying on the internet is an increasing problem worldwide and causes harm to a lot of people often with traumatising effects. There have been several cases where students have dropped out of school as a result, left with emotional wounds that never heal. Schools need to take action, interview the parties involved and listen carefully to the victim, but also to the bully, and ensure a process where the victim can feel safe. An ongoing discussion is whether restorative meetings can be used as an alternative or a supplement to other measures used by the school. We do not have any clear answer to this, but restorative approaches have been used for more than 20 years (Thompson and Smith, 2011, Lyng and Eriksen, 2015), and have been tried out in high schools in Norway. Empirical evidence demonstrates that all parties affected by the bullying responded positively to the outcome of the restorative process, but we must emphasise that we do not take a firm stand on this. To participate in a restorative process is voluntary. We would like to add the following: if circle time or dialogue workshops are used systematically in class throughout the year, there seems to be less bullying among teens.

CASE
Facebook

Saima, 15

Saima is a student in 10th grade (15 years old). Her friend Sara has informed Saima that their friend Ali has published some private photos of her on Facebook. Ali has been Saima's friend since they started in the same class. And now everybody in class is preoccupied with the photos published on the internet. There are many rumours saying that Saima is Ali's girlfriend. A boy named Martin was especially active in spreading this rumour. Saima is afraid her brothers will hear and get involved because of these rumours and that her parents will hear of the photos. Saima contacts the counsellor, who also speaks with Ali, who is surprised by the fuss caused by the photos, but agrees to participate in a restorative meeting. Saima also agrees to participate in a restorative meeting. In addition to Saima, Sara, Martin and the class prefect, Hawra, a peer mediator and a teacher agree to participate. Individual preparatory meetings with all the participants are conducted. In such cases usually a lot of students and onlookers would like to participate, and it is therefore important only to invite those who are directly involved or affected by the incident in order to avoid escalating the incident. The counsellor, who is a mediator, facilitates the meeting. Saima's and Ali's parents have been informed about the incident and were invited to participate in the meeting, but they declined. However, they encouraged and supported the two young people to meet and settle the dispute, and they asked that they be informed of the outcome of the meeting.

The restorative meeting was conducted as planned and the case ended well. The two main parties came up with suggestions on how to solve the situation. An agreement was made on how to interact in the future. The main parties wanted the facilitator to inform parents and class mates that the case was solved and that Saima and Ali were friends again.

Why did this case turn out so well? In our experience the key to success is that the main parties get the opportunity to speak face to face, listen to each other's story, feelings and needs and take on the responsibility for solving the issue. It is a reminder that the two parties know where the hurt is and know the solution. And it is just as important to find good support persons who can follow up informally and prevent bad things from happening. We as facilitators must have the courage to bring people together and lead the process restoratively..

Who should participate in the restorative meeting?

This must be decided on depending on the case. Sometimes the whole class should participate, and in other cases only the victim and the offender and possibly supporting persons for the parties should be involved. Who should facilitate/do the preparations? Should it be a teacher or someone else? Many schools have employees with competence in restorative approaches for handling conflicts; it could be a school mediator, a social worker or others. In some severe cases the police are present. Thorough preparations can ensure that the problem is solved; bad and incomplete preparations can lead to the problems continuing or even increasing. 'Mediation is a process that goes through the following phases' (Zehr, 2002):

Conflict situation – mapping out the conflict – preparations and planning – carrying out the mediation, restorative meeting of dialogue circle – written agreement – follow up.

The central parties are informed that they can bring a support person. This gives the parties a sense of security and ensures that the parties keep the agreement.

PREPARATIONS FOR A RESTORATIVE MEETING

Mapping the situation is important and individual preparatory meetings are the key to a productive meeting and a good result. The preparatory meeting is held with the main parties in the case first, and then the others involved in the case. The main persons can bring their support person and they must be informed of the purpose of the meeting and the form of the meeting. We normally use two facilitators who plan the meeting and who conduct the meeting together:

- The time, place and who is invited to the meeting is decided.

- The participants should be placed seated in a circle. Organise the meeting by placing the chairs in a circle and put names on the seats.

- Plan how the facilitators should open the meeting: start by saying welcome and praise the participants for coming to the meeting.

- In which order should the participants talk? This should be planned before the meeting. In this case it is natural that Saima starts.

- When the participants have reached a result all can accept it is natural for the facilitator to ask if he or she shall inform others of the meeting – their classmates, for example – since everyone has been engaged in what has happened.

- Thank everyone for contributing in a positive way and close the meeting by having everyone shake hands with each other.

We repeat the restorative questions
Talk about:

- What has happened?

- What did you think at the time? What do you think now?

- Who is affected by the incident/situation?

- How do you feel about what happened?

- What has been difficult for you?

- Who is responsible for setting things right?

- What is needed to make things right again?

It can be necessary to follow up with more questions. Here are some suggestions:

- How did your parents react when they heard what happened/ is happening?

- Is there something you need to inform others of from this meeting?

- What can be done to ensure that this does not happen again?

If the restorative meeting is about one specific incident or situation where one or more persons who have admitted 'guilt' sit in the circle, give them positive feedback for having the courage to participate. Always look for possibilities for reintegration.

The restorative meeting ends with a written agreement – the participants sign and schedule a follow-up meeting to ensure the parties are okay and that the agreement is kept. Important questions you must ask are: How is it going with the agreement? How are the parties doing now?

FREQUENTLY ASKED QUESTIONS

Can all types of cases be dealt with in restorative meetings?

Some schools are hesitant to deal with incidents happening outside school, and what goes on on the internet is not a school matter. The media, which has been preoccupied with cases of bullying lately, asks why schools are hesitant to take on the responsibility for handling violations on the internet. Who is responsible for helping young adults in cases such as Saima's?

Others will maintain that it is never dangerous to talk together, but there is no right answer as we see it. Every case must be handled individually, but it is important to remember that young adults meet in school and outside of school – and the perspective of time is important when it comes to handling incidents of violations, such as described in the previous cases. Young adults are impatient and if things take too long according to their perspective, the situation may escalate and more people may get involved, both young adults and parents, and maybe also school leaders. Restorative meetings may not be enough as the only measure, but can be seen as a supplement to other measures such as traditional sanctions, the police or social health care and the school nurse.

THE MICRO CIRCLE

It is a well-known fact that children and young adults quarrel a lot – about small things. A typical argument can, for instance, take place when they are playing, in the schoolyard or in the classroom. Arguments about who sits where in the classroom, and statements such as 'don't touch me' or 'I had it first' are typical for many children when they play, as are fights over who will work together on a school assignment.

The situation may quickly escalate unless the classroom teacher intervenes and stops the fighting. But is that enough to stop the fight or will the disagreement rise again? A lot of adults will recognise the situation where they have exhausted all possible strategies to handle the fighting between students, or their own children, without a good outcome. Inspired by Dominic Barter we have learnt an alternative method for resolving conflicts.

Dominic Barter is the director of the Brazilian Restorative Justice pilot projects, in collaboration with the United Nations Development Programme, United Nations Educational, Scientific and Cultural Organization (UNESCO) and the Brazilian Ministry of Justice, and he has for numerous years worked with Nonviolent Communication and restorative circles. He has introduced the concept of 'micro circles', or 'bare feet' mediation. The method is simple and can be used in all cases and every arena, even in minor conflicts in schools. The micro circle is an easy method where the purpose is to have the two fighting parties talk to each other, then and there, about what has happened, about their needs, and then come up with suggestions of how to go on. The teacher facilitates a quick mediation so that the students one at a time explain what made them angry and come up with fair solutions. By posing restorative questions and follow-up questions the teacher facilitates a simple dialogue with the students – and has the students solve their dispute themselves. It works.

Often it can be sufficient for a child to tell their story while others listen and for them to apologise to each other there and then.

Conflict mediators in different arenas worldwide have been inspired to use micro circles by the work of Dominic Barter (www. restorativecircles.org). In her blog (www.improvecommunication.net), the psychologist Elaine Shpungin says that:

1. The method is quick and focus is on the 'here and now' (takes only a few minutes).

2. The method does not demand that you are very patient, concentrated, creative, understanding, impartial, just or empathic (in the moment).

3. The method strengthens the children's self-assertiveness.

4. The method seem to restore 'harmony' between the children – instead of leaving one child with a sense of injustice and vengeance.

Step 1 Create a space
Take a deep 'calm down breath' and stop the quarrelling as soon as possible if you think it will escalate. Create a physical space between the parties if necessary.

Step 2 Mutual understanding
The children take turns explaining what they want the other to know, while the other reflects on his or her understanding of the message.

Your tool for this phase is simply to ask the following questions:

• What to do you want X to know?

• What do you want to hear Y say to you?

• Is this all?

Ask the exact same questions to both children; one child listens while the other speaks and vice versa. After each child has been heard it is very likely that they are capable of listening to each other and reflecting on what they have heard. Check that each child feels understood.

Step 3 Take action
As soon as you have checked that both children feel they have been heard and understood, make *them* find a solution while you step aside and hold back and enjoy hearing that the children can solve the issue themselves.

The tool for this part is simple:

- Do any of you have a suggestion of how to solve this?
- Is this okay with you?

CASE
Micro circle

Students Eva and John, grade 10, are playing basketball

Eva: 'Teacher, I'm not allowed to join the game. John is so stupid.'

Teacher: 'John, can you please come over here a minute?' 'Eva, *what is it that you want John, to know?*'

Eva: 'I want to play basketball with you!'

Teacher: 'John, *what is it you hear Eva saying?*'

John: [rolling his eyes and sounding insulted]: 'She wants to play with us. But...'

Teacher: [poses a clarifying question to Eva]: 'Stop for a moment, John. Eva, *is it what you want? Is this what you want John to know?*'

Eva: 'Yes.'

(This is the first round – with Eva. Now the same question is asked of John.)

Teacher: 'Okay, John, *what is it you want Eva to know?*'

John: 'I don't want her to play with us just now. I want to be alone with my friend for a little while. We have not had a chance to play together today until now.'

Teacher: 'Eva, *what is it you hear John telling you?*'

Eva: [answering in an unhappy voice]: 'He wants to play with his friend alone.'

Teacher: 'John, is that it?'

John: 'Yes.'

(This is the end of round 2.)

Teacher: 'Eva, is there something else you want John to know?'

Eva: 'No.'

Teacher: John, is there anything else you want Eva to know?'

John: 'No.'

(This concludes the part on mutual understanding. Now how to proceed from here?)

Teacher: 'Thank you, John. Now does anyone have any suggestions as to how you can solve the problem?'

Eva: 'No.'

John: 'Well, she can play with us if she stops asking so many questions about the game.'

Teacher: 'Eva, John says you can play with them if you stop asking so many questions about the game. Is that okay with you?'

Eva: [answers, seemingly happy]: 'Yes.'

Teacher: 'Great! Thank you children.'

This way of communication can be suitable in other settings with older children and teenagers, and even adults, because it is about the basic human needs for understanding and being heard, understanding and being understood.

The systematic use of circles is a way of working proactively with conflict resolution that doesn't cost any money and is not dependent upon external competence. The resource is already there as everyone has it, both staff and students.

FOSTERING STUDENT WELLBEING – A WHOLE-SCHOOL APPROACH

The teenage years are a period of life when young people experience stress, and difficulties with coping and keeping up. Young adults are vulnerable and can often lose a sense of direction in life. The term 'generation perfect' pops up in media and in articles. Many young people struggle in life with loneliness, sadness, social anxiety and depression, and they feel a strong pressure to be 'perfect', be popular, look good and do well in school. The pressure may turn school days into demanding performances, with the result that some young people develop a negative self-image, achieve less well academically and even drop out altogether. We know that a lot of young people do not feel a sense of belonging in school (PISA, 2015), something that is a paradox when we consider that school should be the most important arena when growing up. How can schools and school leaders work to create a healthy learning environment in schools? There is not one answer to this question, but research show that schools that work with a long-term perspective systematically show positive results both academically and socially.

The use of circles encourages creativity and problem-solving, and allows for leaders to step forward but not at the expense of others. When circles are used systematically in daily and/or weekly routines they promote students' self-esteem, self-awareness and empowerment: basic needs that foster students' wellbeing. According to a survey by the Nordic Institute for studies in Innovation, Research and Education (NIFU 2014–2019) school teachers have a strong desire to work systematically to promote good psychological health. A project in kindergarten focuses on the use of circles as a preventive network for children at risk in kindergartens.

A whole-school approach to systematic use of the circle method both in times of peace and conflict can contribute to strengthening social skills and academic learning, and contribute to preventing conflict escalation and reducing the frequency of bullying.

It is the school's responsibility to collaborate with parents to create an inclusive, safe and positive learning environment for all students, and it is the responsibility of the adults to create good relations between students and teachers and between students. This is work with a long-term perspective and it needs to be systematic. The school's mandate is not only to give young people academic or practical skills, it is also to make the students into democratic citizens and provide them with *life skills*. By sharing our ideas and experiences in restorative practices with teachers and others who work with children and young adults we hope to inspire the use of restorative circles and contribute to fostering wellbeing and improving young people's life skills.

Part 4

Games and Activities

These activities have been gathered over many years, so it is difficult to give any references. Most of the activities were learnt at a course with Leap, Wolf & Water, The Mediation Service, Norway, Klinsj and the Center for Conflict Resolution.

CHECK-IN

Time: 10 minutes

Purpose: 'Warm up', get everyone moving, ice breaker. The check-in can also be used to have the participants tune in to the topic for the lesson. A check-in is the start to a lesson where every participant is seen and heard

What to do:

- Tailor the topic according to age and size of the group. The topic should be something that everyone can say something about. Do the round with the sun, remember the talking piece.

- An example of a topic could be:

  - Name one thing you like about your school.

  - Name something you like to do and something you do not like to do.

  - Name one thing you look forward to today.

  - How did you get to school today?

  - Name one person you admire.

  - I feel respected when... I do not feel respected when...

FRUIT SALAD

Time: 10 minutes

Purpose: Have fun and do a little physical activity

What to do:

- Everyone sits in a circle, one chair is removed, and one person sits in the middle. The person in the middle gives every participant the name of a fruit one at a time; for example, apple, pear, plum and banana. The person in the middle calls one type of fruit, for instance, 'apples'. Then all the 'apples' must move to another chair. Rule: You cannot just move to the chair next to where you were sitting.

THE SUN SHINES ON...

Time: 10 minutes

Purpose: Move, laughter and to get to know each other

What to do:

- The group sits on chairs and the chairs are placed in a circle. Remove one chair, so that there is one chair too few. The person without a chair stands in the middle and says: 'The sun shines on you and me and all who are here and who have: dark hair, were sleepy this morning, have siblings, like pizza,' etc. Note that there should only be one description at a time and what is said must be true for the person standing in the middle. All who fit the description must stand up and find a new chair to sit on. The one who is too slow in finding a new place in which to sit will be the next person to stand in the middle and say who the sun shines on.

As the group feels safer, one can challenge them by, for instance, asking them to try the game with feelings, (such as 'I feel hurt when...'), opinions ('I think that...') or skills ('I am good at...'). Examples could be: 'The sun shines on me and all of those who: like to dance, have been so angry they have cried, are engaged with environmental questions. This way the students will get to know each other better.

HURRICANE

Time: 10 minutes

Purpose: Some movement and energy. Break 'old' patterns

What to do:

- The teacher explains how the activity works: when the teacher calls 'hurricane', all the students should find a new place to sit in the group.

- Teacher calls 'hurricane' and everyone finds a new place to sit.

POSITIVE NAME GAME

Time: 15 minutes

Purpose: Play a game, learn a name, ice breaker and establish a positive atmosphere in the group

What to do:

- The group sits on chairs in a circle. One person starts by saying his or her name and a positive adjective that begins with the same letter of his or her first name. For example: 'Active Anne'. The one sitting next to Anne repeats Anne's name and the adjective before he says his or her own name; for instance 'Brave Benny'. And so the round continues, the next person repeats the name and adjective of the person sitting next to him or her before saying his or her own name and an adjective.

- The activity may be made more difficult by saying everyone's names and adjectives before saying his or her own name and adjective.

Make sure that all the adjectives are positive, as negative adjectives will destroy the positive community feeling you are trying to build in the group.

HI, HI, HI

Time: 10 minutes

Purpose: Speed and fun, physical movement, create energy

What to do:

- All participants, except for one, stand in a circle facing inwards. The participant outside the ring walks around the ring, and tickles randomly one person standing in the circle on the back. The person that is tickled must step out of the ring and run around the ring the opposite way to the person who tickled them. When the two meet they must shake hands and say the words: 'Hi, hi, hi!' And then run as fast as possible to get into the empty space in the ring. The one who comes back first, gets a place in the ring, and the other must go and tickle someone else on the back. It is a good idea to play the game until everyone has done a round.

FOUR CORNERS – AN ACTIVITY ON MORAL DILEMMAS

Time: Around 20 minutes

Purpose: Create a discussion and increase the awareness of the topics that are being discussed, present different views on a topic and realise that it is okay to disagree.

Equipment: Four sheets of paper on which it says: AGREE, DISAGREE, PARTIALLY AGREE, PARTIALLY DISAGREE

Alternatives: Four sheets of paper on which it says WRONG, VERY WRONG, QUITE WRONG, NOT WRONG

What to do:

- Place the four sheets of paper in each corner of the room. The person leading the process reads assertions related to the school's rules, and the participants move to the corner they feel fits their point of view, whether they agree, disagree, partially agree or partially disagree. The facilitator asks one person from each group to present his or her point of view. Ask open-ended follow-up questions.

Suggested topics:

- There is a correlation between rules and a positive environment.

- It is just that everyone is treated equally.

- Notices work well.

- It is okay to be late for school.

- It is okay to smoke cigarettes in school.

- If I see someone stealing something in school it is not my responsibility to say something.

What is really good about this activity is that it makes people take a stand, and everyone can state their opinion by moving around to the corners of the room. That way the students participate without having to speak. The activity is easy and it gives room for discussion. It is also good to illustrate that things are not black and white. You are allowed to change your opinion after having heard the others' arguments.

Questions for reflection

- What should students be responsible for?

- What should teachers be responsible for?

BREAK THE CODE

Time: 15 minutes

Purpose: Investigate codes for group making

What to do:

- Three participants leave the room.

- The group that remains in the room makes groups of three to five people based on something they have in common (e.g. the way they sit, similar clothes, same hair style or colour, etc.)

- Ask the ones who are outside to come in one by one. Their task is to find out where they should sit: in which group do they belong? When the 'outsiders' enter the room no-one is allowed to speak.

Reflection

- How did you feel when entering the room?

- What is the relevance to real-life situations?

- What is the basis of groups in school?

- What kind of group are you part of?

- What decides whether you can be part of a group or not?

THE DOT

Time: 15 minutes

Purpose: Feel the sense of belonging to a group and of being kept out of it

Equipment: Dots in different colours, one for each student

What to do:

- Ask the students to close their eyes. Put a dot on the forehead of each person. Let four or five students have the same colour. One or two students get a colour different from the others.

- Give the instruction that nobody is allowed to talk.

- When every participant has a dot in their forehead, ask them to open their eyes and form groups.

- If asked how to form a group the answer is: It is up to you, the task is to form groups without communicating with words.

- When the groups have found each other you can ask:

  - Do you feel you are in the right group?

  - How did find your group?

- You who stand alone. What colour do you think your dot has? What happened when you approached the other groups?

- How does it feel not to be heard/become part of a group?

- How did you who are in a group feel when someone was left alone?

Reflection

- How can this activity connect to situations in class or in school?

- What decides who is in a group?

- What can be done for those who are 'outside' the group, to help them to be part of a group?

- What can the outsiders do to be part of a group?

COUNTING TOGETHER – 1–2–3

Time: 5 minutes

Purpose: Have fun, warm up for pair work

What to do:

- Make pairs of two. The pair (A and B) shall count to three, each counting an alternate number: A: 1, B: 2, A: 3, etc. The facilitator demonstrates for the participants.

- The pairs count to three. If that goes well, speed up!

- The pairs should replace the number one with a sound. You cannot say the word 'one', but instead utter a sound, for instance, 'moo' – and keep on counting two and three.

- The pairs then replace the number two with a movement, for instance, waving the right hand, and count. Sound, movement and number three, this is repeated again and again.

- Would someone like to share their 'act' with the whole group?

MY TRIGGERS

Time: 20 minutes

Purpose: This activity can be used to acknowledge and reflect on unpleasant emotions.

What to do:

Start by working individually, and then by organising small groups for reflection, for instance, in groups of three. Open reflection in the plenary in the end.

- What makes you feel unsettled and impatient?

- What things/situations irritate you?

- What things/situations make you angry?

- What things/situations make you insecure and scared?

- What kind of behaviour/use of words makes you 'turn off' or withdraw from situations?

PAPER – NOT FLOOR

Time: 30 minutes

Purpose: Rehearse problem-solving, creativity and collaboration

Equipment: Flip chart or big piece of brown paper spread out on the floor

What to do:

- Divide the participants into groups; there should be four people in each group.

- Each group lines up next to a piece of paper.

- The facilitator gives the following instruction: every person in the group should touch the sheet of paper, but not the floor. The facilitator goes around observing and encourages the groups to find solutions to the task.

- Next step: the facilitator folds the paper in half and gives the same instruction as the former instruction: every person in the group should touch the sheet of paper, but not the floor.

- Next step: the facilitator folds the paper in half again and gives the same instruction as before: every person in the group should touch the sheet of paper, but not the floor.

- Next step: the facilitator folds the paper and gives the same instruction as before: every person in the group should touch the sheet of paper, but not the floor. And, in addition: no other help is allowed, such as chairs, tables, etc.

- The facilitator instructs the groups to be creative and listen carefully to the words that are being given in the instructions.

Reflection

- How did you feel being part of this activity?

- Did anyone in the group take the lead? How did you feel about that?

- Can you use some of the experiences from this activity in the group work in class?

LISTENING AT SEVERAL LEVELS

Time: 25 minutes

Purpose: Listen carefully and learn to distinguish between facts, feelings and needs

What to do:

- Ask all the participants to think of a conflict situation they have been in, a situation they found very unpleasant, but that was solved then and there. Give the instruction that the participants should be prepared to share their stories with the others (3 minutes).

- Divide the participants into groups of four or five. In each group they will decide on one person who shares his or her story with the others. Before they start sharing, the other group members get some tasks:

  - One person is to listen very carefully and note the main facts in the story: who was involved, where it happened, what happened, etc.

  - Another person should listen for the narrator's emotional experience from the story.

  - A fourth person will listen for the needs the characters in the story have (10 minutes).

- After the person has told the story, the others are instructed to retell/sum up what they have noted. The narrator may correct the story as it is being retold by the others.

Reflection

- Did it work out okay to listen for specific details in the story?

- Did the emotions and needs become clear in the story?

- Was it necessary to interpret?

- What is it important to listen for in order to meet someone with empathy?

- Facts: would the story be told in a different way by the others involved?

- Are facts objective?

- As you can see, the girl in the drawing has legs. The legs symbolise choices. What alternatives could there be in your situations that meet all the underlying needs?

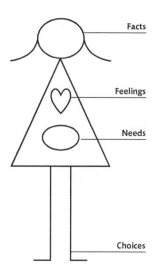

Facts

Feelings

Needs

Choices

THE CONFLICT TREE DIAGRAM

Time: 30 minutes

Purpose: To look into what a conflict is and what causes conflicts

Equipment: A big sheet of paper or poster, marker pens, blackboard or smart board

What to do:

- Draw the trunk of a tree and ask the group the following questions:

  - What is this?

  - What is the trunk without the branches and the leaves?

  - What are conflicts? The group should give examples of conflicts and how they are visible to us. Write down the words on the branches. Write down examples of visible conflicts/signs of conflicts, e.g. war, fights, quarrelling, 'mad dogging' (staring at others). Make sure that exclusion is included too.

- What is necessary for the tree to live? It needs nourishment from the roots. Draw the roots of the tree. The group is asked to give examples of conflicts. There are words that are the answers to these questions:

  - Why are we picking on/yelling at/attacking others?

  - What can be reasons for picking on/yelling at/attacking others? Write down the words on the roots of the tree. Examples can be: jealousy, competition, fear, racism, private family problems, vengeance and insecurity.

Reflection

  - What do you think the reason is for distinguishing between visible signs of conflicts and reasons behind conflicts?

  - What typical conflict situations occur in the classroom?

  - How are they solved in general?

  - Are there other ways of solving conflicts?

  - What type of conflicts are there usually between teenagers/ young adults?

– How do these conflicts occur and how are they (if they are) solved?

LEDERACH: CONFLICT ESCALATION

```
                                                      Separation

                                              Trenches

                                    Enemy

                        Communication ceases

              The problem escalates

        Personal attack/blaming

  Disagreement
```

Time: Around 20 minutes

Purpose: Exercise in conflict analysis. Identify emotions and needs in conflicts.

What to do:

- Teacher tells a story of a conflict

  – Teacher introduces the conflict escalation model

  – Students brainstorm and try to identify steps and place them in the model

  – Students in small groups come up with suggestions as to how the conflict could be de-escalated in the various steps

Reflection

  – Work in small groups

  – How is this model useful in a school context?

ZIP, ZAP, BOP

Time: 15 minutes

Purpose: Laugh together. Reflect on the significance of body language

What to do:

- Everybody stands in a ring facing inwards. An imaginary ball of energy is passed between the participants. The imaginary ball can be sent in the following way:

  - Zip: Hands together and pointing at (and looking at) the person next to you when the word 'Zip!' is uttered. A zip can only be sent sideways in the opposite direction from where it came.

  - Bop: You can bop a zip by lifting both hands with the palms of your hands lifted towards the person the bop aims at, and saying 'Bop!'. Then the zip will change course. You cannot bop a bop, only a zip can be bopped.

  - Zap: When you zap, the imaginary energy ball is sent through the ring. You zap by clasping both hands together and stretching out your arms. The receiver of a zap cannot bop, only zap or zip to another person.

Try it for a couple of rounds and try to increase the speed and raise the level of energy!

The activity, 'Zip, Zap, Bop' evolves further by omitting the sounds (not saying 'Zip', 'Zap', 'Bop') and just using the hand gestures. Then the next step could be not using the hand gestures and only communicating by using eye movements. Here you can add further details to the story by introducing characters such as spies and secret agents.

Reflection

- Can you think of examples from your everyday life where you would use zips, zaps and bops?

- What is a bop really?

- How does it feel to receive a bop?

- 'As a teacher my experience of getting a bop...' (use examples of when you have experienced rejection; for example, negative body language when you are about to explain something important in class, such as a problem in mathematics or English grammar that you have prepared well).

'I' MESSAGE AND 'YOU' MESSAGE (GIRAFFE AND JACKAL LANGUAGE)

Time: 45 minutes

Purpose: Present Marshall Rosenberg's Nonviolent Communication model. Practise conflict reducing language

What to do:
It is important that the facilitator is familiar with the theory of Nonviolent Communication and knows the model well. In addition to books on the Nonviolent Communication model there are videos and a lot of material on the internet.

In short: Rosenberg uses the giraffe as a symbol of Nonviolent Communication. The giraffe has a big heart (empathic), long neck (good view) and big ears (good listener). The jackal is the symbol of the type of communication that escalates a conflict. The jackal or the wolf is a smaller animal that sees parts of an incident and interprets the rest; it feels unsafe, barks and attacks.

Nonviolent Communication is a way of communication that focuses both on your own needs and the needs of others. The 'I' message is a way of communicating that is without attack on the other party, criticism, negative interpretations or judgement. The idea is that behind any criticism, judgement or attack there is a person with feelings and needs that have not been met. If and when a person reproaches you, it is a challenge to listen to what unmet needs lie underneath the reproach. Rosenberg encourages us all to listen to what the other party is in need of, instead of what he or she thinks of you.

- Draw a giraffe and a jackal/wolf on a poster or on the blackboard.

- Ask the questions: What do you see here? What is significant about the giraffe, and the jackal?

Write the key words. Ask the group if they have examples from situations where communication has been difficult because of jackal/wolf language? Give names to the conflicts and write them down. Choose one of the examples and have the group find out how the participants could have expressed themselves differently by using giraffe language and giraffe listening strategies. Have the participants make up a short role play to demonstrate how giraffe language works.

Write the four steps of 'I' messages on a poster or on the blackboard:

- Share what you observe – facts.

- How do you experience what you observe?

- What do you need?

- What do you suggest – wish.

You may talk about 'I' messages and 'you' messages and describe how the two forms of communication work in different conflicts.

Have the participants share examples and reflect together, and practise speaking using both forms of communicating.

FOUR SMALL WORDS

Time: 20 minutes, depending on how big the group is

Purpose: Get all the students to actively participate in a debate and at the same time have respect for the opinion of others. Work on the significance of the words that are put forward

Equipment: Paper (poster), pens and marker pens, smart board, blackboard or flip chart.

What to do:

- Ask each student to find four words they think are important for describing a good class environment. The students write their four words on a piece of paper (3 minutes).

- Ask the students to work in pairs. Together the pairs will find a new list of words of four words. No new words are to be added, and no words are to be put together. Give the instruction that the time is nearly up when there is 1 minute left (3 minutes).

- Ask the pairs to join another pair so that they make up groups of four. The group should now discuss the words and decide on four words. Give the instruction that the time is nearly up when there is 1 minute left (3 minutes).

- The group of fours will now join into groups of eight that will end up with four words (3 minutes). And so the activity continues until all the participants are joined in one group.

- Write down the four words on the blackboard or on a poster. Ask everyone to look at the words and confirm that they agree that these are the most important elements for good communication.

The task is well suited for the teaching of many topics. For example: what defines a family, reasons for war, what should be the assessment criteria for oral presentations?

Reflection

- How does it feel to make compromises?

- Was it difficult to find agreements?

- Was it harder when the group got bigger?

- How do you define the various concepts?

- What have you learnt about communication in this process? For example, how do stress/time pressure and disagreements affect the ability to communicate?

- Is there something in the process you can relate to (the) work in class?

WHO IS THE LEADER?

Time: 20 minutes

Purpose: invisible hierarchy in groups

What to do:

- One participant leaves the room.

- The others line up in a circle facing inwards in the circle. They decide on who is the leader.

- When the one who left the room comes back in, the leader starts making a movement; for example, nodding their head, clapping their hands, etc. The others copy the movements of the leader. After some time the leader changes their movements and the others follow and copy.

- The task is for the outsider to discover who the leader is, and for the group to conceal it.

Reflection

- How did you feel when doing this activity?

- What situations could this activity remind you of?

- What does secret leadership do to the school environment? Does it have to be negative?

- What would motivate you to take on leadership of a student group?

PERSONAL ROAD MAP

Time: 40 minutes

Purpose: Get to know one another. Do an individual activity where we share important events from our lives with the group

What to do:

- The students are each given a poster, pens, marker pens and coloured pencils. They are given the task, individually, of drawing a personal road map of their lives until the present day. They can, for instance, use drawings, words and symbols that illustrate choices they have made, periods and incidents in their lives until now (10 minutes).

- The students go into pairs and share their road maps with each other and try to find out/interpret their drawings. Thereafter the owner of the map gives feedback and explanations of their map (10 minutes).

- Back in the circle/in their places they are given the instruction to decide on an incident from the road map they think is significant and positive and which they would like to share with the others. It could be a positive crossroads. Take turns so that everyone shares what they have chosen (15 minutes).

Reflection

- Do the personal roadmaps have anything in common?

- Was it useful to draw the maps? In what way(s)?

- How can what you have learnt help to understand others?

- To what extent can we decide what direction our lives take?

THE MOUNTAIN

Time: 10 minutes

Purpose: Take the temperature of the group, how are they doing together

What to do:

- Each participant gets a copy of the Mountain (see drawing). They must mark the figure that best describes how they feel. If the drawing is used at the beginning of the year you can bring it up again in the spring to see if they mark off some other point at the end of the year.

Reflection

- Where are you compared to the others?

- Is anyone helping you?

- Are you helping someone?

- Why are you where you are?

- Are you somewhere else now compared to the beginning of the year?

- What must happen for you to be one of the other figures in the drawing?

Students who are moving on to apprenticeships can use the drawing as a part of preparing for the transition between school and the apprenticeship. The students can mark how they see themselves as apprentices. *Are you ready for the apprentice role? If not, what do you need to be ready?*

The drawing can also be used for working with psychic health and on Global Dignity Day (https://globaldignity.org/global-dignity-day).

THE MUG

Time: 5 minutes

Purpose: To have the group see things from different angles and that there are 'many' truths

What to do:

- The facilitator holds a cup with a logo or a drawing on it. The group members are seated in a way so that each group member sees parts of the mug (some placed in front, some placed at the back and some placed at the sides). Ask the group to describe what they see.

Reflection

- Who is right?

- Is there more than one answer?

- How many solutions did the group come up with?

- What if there had only been two sides?

WHAT IS HIDDEN BEHIND ANGER?

Time: 20 minutes

Purpose: Create awareness of the connection between anger and emotions and needs/emotional needs. Encourage the participants to reflect on and express what is behind their emotions

What to do:

- Ask the participants to write down a sentence that describes a situation when they were really angry. One example could be: 'I was angry when my contribution to the meeting was ignored'.

- Explain that often grief or hurt feelings lie underneath anger. Ask the participants to write a sentence about the hurt feelings behind the anger in the situations they were thinking of. For instance: 'I was hurt because it seemed as if no-one took my opinion on the matter seriously'.

- Explain that the reason for being hurt that way is often needs that are not satisfied. Ask everyone to spend 2 minutes writing a sentence on the needs they had in this situation. For instance: 'I have a need to be valued and accepted by my colleagues'.

- In addition to needs that are not met, you should explain that fear is often present when we get angry. Ask the participants to spend 2 minutes thinking of what they feared in the situation of anger and write a sentence about it. For example: 'I am afraid that I will not be respected by my colleagues'.

- The participants find a partner they can share their sentences with (6 minutes).

RESTORATIVE QUESTIONS

Time: 60 minutes

Purpose: Model communication without attacks, criticism, judgement or interpretation. The questions are used in mediation processes, both in the initial meetings and the mediation/restorative justice meeting. It is a great tool in any setting

What to do:

- Can be used in all individual meetings related to conflict resolution.

Talk about:

- What happened?
- Who is affected and how?
- How did you experience what happened?
- What is needed to put things right?
- What would you suggest?
- What is needed in order for this never to happen again?

CHECK-OUT – EVALUATION

Time: 10 minutes

Purpose: To evaluate the outcome of a workshop, schoolwork, class, instruction, etc.

What to do:

- Make an imaginary diagonal cross in the classroom or a suitable space.

- How did you enjoy this class?

- What are you especially proud of from this class/today?

- How content are you with the instructional methods or ways of working in this class/today?

- Spread out four sheets diagonally in the classroom. On each piece of paper the following is printed: HIGHLY SATISFIED, SATISFIED, A BIT SATISFIED, NOT SATISFIED. The teacher can also be more specific and ask questions related to the curriculum or the assessment criteria. The students then place themselves according to the sheet of paper that they feel is right.

Reflection

- Can you say specifically what you are dissatisfied with/satisfied with? What do you wish to be better at? What can you do in order to become better? What do you need from the teacher to get better?

GIVE A COMPLIMENT

Time: 5–10 minutes

Purpose: Practise giving each other positive feedback

What to do:

- All participants stand in a circle. The person to the right of the facilitator is asked to stand in the middle of the circle facing the instructor, who gives the person in the middle a compliment. It could be that one person has done a really good job in class, or simply: 'I like your smile'.

- NB: please remind the participants that the purpose is to be to the point, say something positive and avoid saying: 'I *think* you are a good guy', as an example. Then do the round one by one, the next student changes place with the person who has been given a compliment, the person to the left of the facilitator can now be given a compliment. Each person given a compliment receives a clap.

TAP ON THE SHOULDER
The facilitator starts by giving the person sitting to the left a friendly look and a tap on the shoulder, and says: 'Have a good day!'

THE PYRAMID OF CONFIRMATION/ ACKNOWLEDGEMENT
One at a time the participants are instructed to: say something positive about today's workshop, activity and put your hand on top of a pyramid – just like you see in team sports. When everyone has said their word and the pyramid is concluded, finish off by everyone shouting 'Hey!', and just after this the pyramid is dissolved.

TEXAS HUG
Time: 1 minute

Purpose: Positive conclusion, feeling of community

What to do:

- All stand in a circle and hold their arms on each others' shoulders. Everyone takes a step back and two big steps into the circle while shouting 'Whoa!', so that the group members end up in a big group hug.

JUMP TOGETHER
Time: 5 minutes

Purpose: Concentration and community-building

What to do:

- All the participants stand in a circle, with space between each person. The participants are instructed to do a long jump into the circle when the facilitator gives the signal. No talking or noises are allowed. Underline that it is important to wait until everyone is quiet before beginning the activity so they can 'feel' the others around them. It could be that more than one attempt is necessary, but it always works out in the end. Somehow this also works well with very large groups.

Bibliography

Costello, B., Wachtel, J. and Wachtel, T. (2010) *Restorative Circles in Schools: Building Community and Enhancing Learning.* Bethlehem, PA: International Institute of Restorative Practices.

Christie, N. (1977) *Conflict as Property.* Oslo: University of Oslo.

Christie, N. (2009) *Små ord for store spørsmål.* Oslo: Universitetsforlaget.

Dewey, J. (1916) *Democracy and Education: An Introduction to the Philosophy of Education.* Renewed by John Dewey (1944). New York: The Free Press.

Drugli, M.B., Klökner, C., and Larsson, B. (2011) 'Do demographic factors, school functioning, and quality of student–teacher relationships as rated by teachers predict internalising and externalising problems among Norwegian school children?' *Evaluation and Research in Education, 24*(4), 243–254.

Elevundersøkelsen (2015) Student survey. Available at https://www.udir.no/tall-og-forskning/finn-forskning/rapporter/elevundersokelsen-2015--hovedrapporten/ (accessed 23 August 2018).

Eriksen, I. and Lyng, S. (2015) 'Schools' alternative strategies for fostering a sound psychosocial environment.' *Norwegian Centre for Social Research.* Available at www.hioa.no/eng/About-HiOA/Centre-for-Welfare-and-Labour-Research/NOVA/Publikasjonar/Rapporter/2015/Schools-alternative-strategies-for-fostering-a-sound-psychosocial-environment (accessed 24 May 2018).

Freire, P. [1968] (1970) *The Pedagogy of the Oppressed.* New York: Bloomsbury.

Gordon, T. (1979) *T.E.T. Teacher Effectiveness Training.* Norwegian edition. Oslo: Dreyer forlag.

Galtung, J. (2003) *Peace by Peaceful Means.* London: Sage Publications.

Halstensen, S. (2016) 'Dialogsirkelen og innagerende atferd. En kvalitativ undersøkelse av læreres erfaring med dialogverksted som verktøy for å fremme gode relasjoner' ['Dialogue circle and introvert behaviour. A qualitative survey of teachers' experience with dialogue workshop as a tool for promoting positive relations'] (own translation). Master's dissertation.

Hattie, J. (2008) *Visible Learning – A Synthesis of Over 800 Meta-Analysis Relating to Achievement.* London: Routledge.

Hattie, J. (2012) *Visible Learning for Teachers. Maximizing Impact on Learning.* New York: Routledge.

Hopkins, B. (2011) *The Restorative Classroom: Using Restorative Approaches to Foster Effective Learning.* London: Optimus Education.

Hopkins, B. (2013) *Just Schools: A Whole School Approach to Restorative Justice.* London and Philadelphia, PA: Jessica Kingsley Publishers.

Johnstone, G. (2002) *Restorative Justice – Ideas, Values, Debates.* Cullompton, Devon: Willan Publishing.

Karlsen, C.R. (2016) 'Stille elever i dialog. Hvilke erfaringer hare lever som viser innagerende atferd med deltakelse i dialog verksted? 'Camilla Ruud Karlsen (2016) 'The Quiet students in Dialogue. What experiences do quiet students have in participating in a dialogue workshop?' Available at https://www.duo.uio.no/bitstream/handle/10852/52091/1/Camilla-Ruud-Karlsen-innagerende-atferd-og-dialogverksted.pdf (accessed 23 August 2018).

Lederach, P. (2005) *The Moral Imagination.* Oxford: Oxford University Press.

Lovdata (1991) *Lov om konfliktrådsbehandling (konfliktrådsloven) [Law on conflict management (the Conflict Act)]* Available at https://lovdata.no/dokument/NL/lov/2014-06-20-49?q=konfliktrådloven (accessed 31 August 2018).

Lund, I. (2008) 'I just sit there: shyness as an emotional and behavioural problem at school.' *Journal of Research in Special Educational Needs, 8*(2), 78–87.

Lyng S.T. and Eriksen I.M. (2015) *Schools alternative strategies for fostering a sound psychosocial environment.* Available at http://www.hioa.no/eng/About-HiOA/Centre-for-Welfare-and-Labour-Research/NOVA/Publikasjonar/Rapporter/2015/Schools-alternative-strategies-for-fostering-a-sound-psychosocial-environment (accessed 23 August 2018).

NIFU (2014–2019) *Psykik helse i skolen.* Available at https://www.udir.no/globalassets/upload/forskning/2014/psykisk-helse.pdf (accessed 10 September 2018).

O'Moore, M. (2010) *Understanding School Bullying: A Guide for Parents and Teachers.* Dublin: Veritas Publications.

Pranis, K. (2005) *The Little Book of Circle Process: A New/Old Approach to Peacemaking.* New York: Good Books.

Rosenberg, M.B. (2003) *Nonviolent Communication: A Language of Life.* Encinitas, CA: PuddleDancer Press.

Rubin, H.K., Wojslawowicz, J.C., Krasnor, L.R., Booth-LaForce, C. and Burgess, K.B. (2006) 'The best friendships of shy/withdrawn children: prevalence, stability, and relationship quality.' *Journal of Abnormal Child Psychology, 34*(2), 139–153.

Skåland, B. (2016) 'The experience of student-to-teacher violation: A phenomenological study on Norwegian teachers being violated by students'. PhD dissertation. Norwegian University of Science and Technology, available at https://brage.bibsys.no/xmlui/handle/11250/2382336 (accessed 26 July 2018)

Thapa, A., Cohen, J., Guffrey, S. and Higgins-D'Alessandro, A. (2013) 'A review of school climate research.' *Review of Educational Research, 83*(3), 357–385.

Thompson, F. and Smith, P.K. (2011) *The Use and Effectiveness of Anti-bullying Strategies in Schools.* Goldsmiths, University of London, UK. Report commissioned by the Department of Education. Available at https://www.gov.uk/government/publications/the-use-and-effectiveness-of-anti-bullying-strategies-in-schools (accessed 24 May 2018).

Vygotsky, L. (1934) *Thought and Language.* Cambridge, MA: MIT Press.

Wachtel, T. (1998) *Real Justice: How We Can Respond to Wrongdoing.* Bethlehem, PA: Piper's Press.

Wachtel, T. and Costello, B. (2009) *The Restorative Practices Handbook.* Bethlehem, PA: International Institute for Restorative Practices.

Weale, S. (2017) 'Restorative justice in UK schools could help reduce exclusion', *The Guardian,* 29 December.

World Health Organization (2017) Statistics. Available at http://www.who.int/mental_health/prevention/suicide/suicideprevent/en (accessed 23 August 2018).

Zehr, H. (2002) *The Little Book of Restorative Justice.* Brattleboro, VT: Good Books.

INTERNET RESOURCES

Advocates for Youth
  www.advocatesforyouth.org/workingwithyouth/43?task=view
  https://antibullyingcentre.ie/bullying/cyberbullying
Barter, D. Culture of Empathy
  http://cultureofempathy.com/References/Experts/Dominic-Barter.htm
Barter, D. On Restorative Circles
  https://www.youtube.com/watch?v=bazgiTyieKo
  https://www.circle-time.co.uk
Edutopia
  www.edutopia.org
Improve Communication
  www.improvecommunication.net
International Institute for Restorative Practices
  https://www.iirp.edu
Murray White Publications and Resources
  www.murraywhite-selfesteem.co.uk/pubres.htm
Odinstiftelsen
  www.odinstiftelsen.no
PISA Report 2015
  www.oecd.org/pisa

European Forum for Restorative Justice
www.euforumrj.org
Restorative Circles
https://www.restorativecircles.org
www.restorativeschools.org.nz/
Mona O'Moore (2016)
https://www.slideshare.net/iktsenteret/cyberbullying-digitalmobbing-06042016-mona-omoore
UNICEF – Convention on the Rights of the Child
www.unicef.org/crc
Safe Learning
http://trygglaring.no/en/home-2/
School Project, Maine, Restorative Works
https://www.iirp.edu/news/2482-maine-schools-report-positive-preliminary-result
Swedish Forum for Mediation and Conflict Resolution
www.s-f-m.se
Transforming Conflict
www.transformingconflict.org
Trygg Læring, Norway
www.trygglaring.no

Index